The Serendipities
of a
Mother's Prayers

Gordon Barnett

PHIL 3:12

The Serendipities of a Mother's Prayers

Gordon Barnett

This is a story of a fascinating journey to redemption for a Navy Commander. This is a chronicle of God's grace.

To order additional copies of this book, contact:
Xlibris Corporation
1-888-795-4274
www.Xlibris.com
Orders@Xlibris.com
72873

Contents

Dedication

To Elida, my companion, advisor, encourager, best friend, helpmate, coheir, lover, and wife, with whom I am blessed. You bring out the best and forgive the worst. With all that I am and all that I ever will be, this is wholly dedicated to you.

Foreword

My prayers used to be "O God, do something about my dad."
Now I pray, "O Lord, make me more like my dad."

Dennis Barnett

Acknowledgement

Joel Martinez, a missionary in Granada, Spain, after hearing many of my stories, urged me to write a book telling others. He and his wife, Nancy, have a growing ministry to the Spanish people.

Endorsements

Gordon Barnett is a man who was rescued by the prayers of a Godly mother, and his story is one you will never forget. Without his knowing it or deserving it, the favor of God was resting upon him, protecting him, enabling him, advancing him, because his mother refused to give up on the dream she had for her son. That dream was Heaven's ultimate plan for Gordon, and now he is living it to the fullest, by the grace of God. This book will help you never to give up on anyone. Maybe even yourself! —Dr. David C Walker, my Pastor

"Few people experience a life such as Gordon Barnett's. Fewer still are able to write such a colorful and accurate account. From boyhood to senior years, there is the indelible print of a godly heritage. Through success and frustration, the Lord ultimately exposes His plan by sealing his salvation with the evidence of marital satisfaction and true soul joy. Remarkable accomplishments of his personal life fade in the light of saving grace."—Dr. Orval C. Butcher

"Gordon is a great pilot, a better leader, a humble human, a loving husband, an adopted father to my wife, and a grandfather to my girls, a true friend and model to me. "He is also one who could run his life better than anyone and proceeded to run it into the ground. Above all else, Gordon is an example of God's grace working to redeem . . . And boy, did redemption work! Be blessed as you read." —William Eddy, Missionary in Spain

"My dad and I have a loving and respectful relationship today. It wasn't always this case. When I was a child, there were times when my dad made mistakes, and for a long time, I harbored resentment for his bad behavior. "When we both got sober through AA in 1984 and found our higher power, our lives changed and so did our relationship. He is a changed man today. Overall, as a father, he was a basically good provider and is currently (eighty-five years young) a healthy and happy man who has a loving and supportive wife, active in his layman evangelical Christian work and missionary support. He is my father, and I love him for who he was, even more for what he has become. "This semiautobiographical book is an ad hoc collection of memories and short stories that my dad has verbally related to friends and family and, with recent encouragement, has put in writing before he leaves this life to be with his Lord in heaven."—Doug Barnett

"Stories of an ordinary man living out extraordinary exploits as a vessel of an awesome God!"
—Elida Barnett, my wife

Prologue

His Eyes Were Brown

December 13, 1945—it was a wintry day in New England. I was stationed at Quonset Point, Rhode Island. My friend and fellow aviator, Kenny Barnes, and I were torpedo pilots in the US Navy's VX-1, an experimental squadron that had twenty-six different kinds of aircraft. Kenny was going to take me for my first flight in the Curtiss SB2C Helldiver. It was only his third flight in this aircraft.

As we were dressing in our winter gear, a sailor stuck his head into the ready room and said, "My wife is having a baby next month. I need one more hour of flight time in order to receive my flight pay."

Since we were the only flight scheduled that day, I let him take my place. One hour later, we received an ominous call from base radio that a Hell Diver was down near Charleston, Rhode Island.

Kenny Barnes had crashed into the rocky slopes near Charleston, Rhode Island. He was making a gunnery run on one of our other aircraft. The first attempt at this risky aerial maneuver was successful. However, when he tried to get back to make another run, he turned too hard, started to spin, got out of the spin, but not out of the dive.

The rescue was initiated immediately. I was a volunteer in the jeep that took us through the woods in search of the crash. The fire was already out when we located the wreckage. I peered at Kenny in the front cockpit. He was a mess.

I removed his charred Navy wings and put them in my pocket.

I knew I would be taking his body home to his widowed bride, Dotty, and three-month-old son, Kenny.

Then I looked at the man in the rear cockpit. He was also dead. I thought to myself, "God, this was the second man to die for me. Why did you spare me?" This would not be the first nor last time I would ask God this question.

I took Kenny's body home to his grieving wife and mother in Cincinnati, Ohio. I transported him on the same train for which he had purchased a ticket to go home for Christmas.

Previously, telegrams were sent to both his mother and widow. When I arrived, it was reported to me that his mother, upon receiving the news, had taken her telegram to her daughter-in-law and greeted her with "The life insurance is all mine." Dotty was not so coldhearted. She replied, "I don't care, I just want my husband back."

I spent the next four days at the funeral home decked out in my Navy ensign's uniform trying to look my somber best, when suddenly I found myself thrust into the middle of a family feud. Many arrived and prayed the rosary around the casket. Dotty and her four brothers, upset over the mother's insurance decision, encountered another disagreement.

When I asked Dotty if she wanted taps at the burial, she really didn't care one way or the other. However, Ken's mother said that she couldn't stand taps and we shouldn't play them. My feelings were obvious. The four brothers overruled the mom and said, "We will have taps."

I suggested to them that if it were me, I would want to have the official presence of honorary military pallbearers. We all agreed that this is how Ken should be honored on that sad day in Cincinnati, Ohio.

Sixty years later, on Father's Day, June 2006, I received the following e-mail from Kenny, the son. He was named after his father.

> Dear Gordon and Elida, Happy Father's Day to you Gordon, as you will soon be a grandfather again; my oldest daughter Karrie Ann Foley will be delivering our first grandchild which will make you a great grandfather, *as I consider you my father.* Karrie wants to know if my Dad had blue or brown eyes. I never asked Mom and I really don't know what color eyes he had. Please e-mail me what you remember!
>
> Hope you are both doing well and wish you a happy and prosperous day on this Father's Day. *You will always be the father I never had.* I always pray every night for both you and Elida. Best regards, from Ken & Maria Barnes! Love ya!

I felt especially honored to become another father and great-grandfather. My reply to Karrie's inquiry was "His eyes were brown."

Chapter 1

From November 29, 1923, to December 8, 1942

First Memories

The first thing that I remember in my life was walking to a country school exactly one mile from our house near Cedar Rapids, Iowa. Glenn, my older brother by twenty-two months, and I walked together on that long lonesome one-mile trek. It seemed a lot farther than a mile since I was only four years old.

In that country school, one teacher taught all eight grades. There was no kindergarten. The eighth-grade girls were adults to me. I recall that I cried very easily. Every time I would cry, one of the motherly eighth graders would pick me up and console me. With such attention, I remember crying a lot.

When it snowed, the walk to school was difficult for us. Glenn would walk ahead of me and make a path in the snow to follow. When the snow was extremely deep, it was even hard for my big brother Glenn.

One day, after about thirty minutes into our trip, I turned around and went back home. I told Mother that it was just too cold. She turned me around, pushed me out of the door, and said, "You are going to school today." Without Glenn, it was a long and lonesome journey.

My next childhood memory was when we lived in the little town of Independence, Iowa. I was in the second grade. I was walking home from school through six-inch snow. Fortunately, this school was only four blocks from our home. I recall crossing the street and not paying much attention. An automobile struck me and threw me ten feet in the air. The next thing I remember was that I was in a hospital, but fortunately, because of divine providence, I was unharmed. However, the vehicle was not so lucky. They told me I had made a large dent in the automobile. This was just one example of my mother's prayers that continue to protect and follow me throughout my life.

I Got His Girl

It was the year 1933. I was ten. The school that we attended was in the country and was across the street from our home.

At school, there was a bully who was twelve. He bullied all of us, and we didn't like it. He made life at school very difficult.

One day after school, I walked with him and his two sisters down the road toward the creek. We were arguing, and finally we broke into a fight.

I got him down and was holding him as I asked him to give up. He begged one of his sisters to get his knife. I held her off. Finally, he gave up.

Word of this got out at the school, and his girlfriend became my girlfriend.

During 1993, while I was visiting my son Dennis who was a Pastor in Independence, Iowa, a couple who used to babysit my younger brothers took us to the home of this girl in La Porte

City, Iowa. I knocked on her door, and we visited for fifteen minutes. She was seventy years old.

Breakfast During the Depression

During the Depression, there were nine people in our family to feed. My father's salary was about eight dollars per month.

My father, the Reverend C. H. Barnett, purchased a bushel of wheat for ten cents. He brought it home. We picked over it on our dining room table, taking out the small stones and other foreign substances.

Then mother put it in shallow pans and roasted it in our wood-burning kitchen stove. Some of the wheat burned.

Dad then took it to a mill where he had it cracked. I believe that it was the original cracked wheat; it was our breakfast for our entire winter.

I have looked for cracked wheat in many grocery stores ever since. Never have I been able to find cereal so delicious.

Cake Frosting

The cake frosting incident happened during 1935. I was twelve. Mother Barnett taught all of her eight children to cook. I was the cake baker. Every Saturday afternoon, I made a cake from scratch. We had no prepared cake mix in boxes during those days.

This particular Saturday, the whole family was gone, and I was alone to prepare the Sunday evening cake for our cake and milk *supper*.

I remember the word *supper*. We don't hear it much anymore. It was a good word. In those days, *dinner* was the noon meal, and *supper* was the evening meal. Now, *dinner* has been changed to *lunch*, and *supper* has been changed to *dinner*. What will they do next?

I prepared the dry ingredients for the cake. I added the eggs and wet ingredients and baked the cake in our kitchen wood-burning stove. It looked and smelled good.

When it was cool, I made the frosting. I used powdered sugar, butter, and water. This time I used the recipe from mother's cookbook. It called for some coffee to moisten the frosting. I could not figure how coffee could moisten the mixture.

I could not find any coffee in the house, but I found some tea leaves. I thought, "That is a good substitute." So I added about a tablespoon of tea leaves.

It looked funny, and I was proud of my work.

When mother came home, she looked at the cake and said, "Gordon, the cake has measles." She was right, it did.

The whole family enjoyed the cake with measles Sunday evening. It did taste good.

Efficacy

It was during the year 1936. I was twelve years old and in the eighth grade. We attended a one-room school three-quarters of a mile from our home. We had one teacher who taught all grades, one through eight. Her name was Dorothea Crane. She not only taught all eight grades, she had to build the fire in the large stove during the winter. She had to carry out the ashes. She had to sweep the floors. She had to clean the black boards. She was paid sixty dollars per month.

She offered me one dollar per month (one nickel per day) to take care of the heat and ashes. I had to walk three-quarters of a mile over the snowdrifts and unlock the schoolhouse door before 8:00 AM daily. I would start the coal fire and stand on top of the stove to heat my feet. During the day, I would bring in more coal and carry out the ashes.

When a student needed to go to the bathroom, he would raise one finger if he wanted to pee, two fingers if he wanted to poop. The toilets, five-hole privies, were about half a block from the schoolhouse door. The boys' privy was in one corner of the schoolyard; the girls' was in the opposite corner.

Our school was to send one student to the county seat as a contestant in the National Spelling Bee. A second-grade girl beat me in our school spell-off. Our teacher thought it would not be right to send a second-grade student; therefore she sent me.

My parents drove me to the county seat in Onawa, Iowa. It was about thirty miles from our home. The large auditorium was full of people.

The first trial was a standing trial. You were to sit down if you failed to spell a word correctly.

When it was my turn, they gave me the word *efficacy*. Wow, I had never heard of that word. They put it in a sentence. It was still a foreign word to me.

I tried to spell it. I had to sit down. I was ashamed, since it was in front of my Mom and Dad.

I learned to spell *efficacy* that day and have never failed to spell it correctly.

I wonder what my second word would have been, had I spelled it correctly.

They Tried to Tip Over the Preacher's Privy

It was during the summer of the year 1938, my brother Glenn and I were home for the summer from a Christian academy in Kansas. My father was the Pastor of the Wesleyan Methodist church in Rudd, Iowa.

We had heard that some of the youth in town were going to tip over our outhouse, a three-hole privy, during that night.

The Barnett boys, just after dark, lifted the privy and moved it four feet forward. We covered the deep hole with sticks, then leaves, and finally dust. Then we waited.

Shortly before midnight, we heard a scream. "Help! Get me out of here!"

The next morning, we moved the privy four feet back. We didn't have to remove the sticks and leaves.

It was not Halloween, but it was our best Halloween ever.

A Runaway

When I reached the age for high school, my parents sent me to a parochial school in Miltonvale, Kansas. It was an especially strict institution. Smoking, drinking, and going to movies were prohibited; public displays of affection were discouraged.

It was a Saturday, January 1938, when Merlin Hodges, a fellow student and an Oklahoma Pastor's son, and I hitchhiked from Miltonvale to Clay Center, Kansas. I was fifteen, Merlin was sixteen. The two towns were about twenty miles apart. We had the grand total of thirty cents between us.

When we arrived in Clay Center, Merlin asked me, "Shall we smoke a cigarette or shall we go to a movie?" I suggested that we go to a movie. I had never been to the movies before. It cost ten cents for a ticket and it was a Western. That's about all I can remember about our so-called sinful behavior.

The following Monday at the school's chapel, C. Floyd Hester, the College Bible School and Academy president made the following draconian announcement in the presence of the whole student body, "Merlin Hodges and Gordon Barnett have committed an immoral act and will be expelled from classes for one week." Someone must have seen us leaving the movie and snitched.

Merlin and I imagined what all of the students suspected, and we were very embarrassed.

After chapel, Merlin and I decided to escape the ridicule, so we packed our little bags and started to hitchhike to California. We went south to Salina, Kansas, then west toward California. We planned to join the Army. It was February 3, 1938. It was very cold.

We had one nickel between us. This trip turned out to be a poorly planned endeavor. We spent the five cents on a Powerhouse candy bar, which we devoured as our only sustenance.

Our last ride dropped us off in the Kansas countryside about midnight. It was February and very cold, with a light sprinkle of snow on the ground. Here we were, all alone in the desolate and dark landscape on a road beside a field full of corn shocks that looked like Indian tepees. We felt tired, cold, lonely, and desperate.

We decided to crawl into one of the shocks of corn. It was warmer, but we still couldn't sleep. It was in that inhospitable corn shock that I decided to go back home and face our punishment.

We then walked back to the closest town and went to the railroad station. Because the town was innocent and trusting in those days, the door was unlocked. We tried to build a fire in the potbelly stove in the station. We found wood, but had no way to light it. Down the tracks about two hundred yards, a lantern on a pole was burning. It was difficult to find a flammable object that I could light and then carry to the stove, but I was finally able to do so. The stove warmed us, but we couldn't lie down on the benches because they had armrests.

We waited until daylight before I began to hitchhike back to our school. I wasn't sure if Merlin was going to follow me. Later that day, I made it back and when I arrived, I ate all the popcorn my roommate had. For my much-feared punishment, I spent the week at one of my professor's home helping his wife perform house chores. My mother's prayers continued to protect and follow me.

My partner in crime (Merlin) made it back soon after my arrival, and believe it or not, although we had a "bad" reputation, we were the most popular students in the school for a few days.

Razor Blades

It was during the year 1940. I was sixteen. We were visiting my Uncle Wallace's family near Lockport, New York.

I bet my cousin, Howard Barnett, twenty-five cents that I could swallow a double-edged razor blade. He quickly took up my challenge.

He gave me the blade. I put it in my mouth. I crunched it between my teeth, and it broke into pieces. I crunched them between my teeth again, and it broke them into many pieces.

When I felt that I had the pieces small enough, I swallowed them. I then ate a slice of bread. He paid me a quarter.

I collected more quarters by this act during my freshman year at Houghton College.

Maybe I was not so smart after all, because twenty-three years later, my colon was completely removed.

Track Shoes

It was in the spring of 1941. My brother Glenn and I were freshmen at Houghton College.

Coach McNease suggested that I probably should run the 440-yard dash in the upcoming track meet where all college classes competed against one another.

I did not know how to run, but I did practice running even when snow was on the track. I ran in my heaviest shoes, because with track shoes, I could go faster. We Barnett boys had no track shoes, for they were expensive.

A fellow student offered to sell us his track shoes for a price that fit our budget. They were too small for me and too large for my brother Glenn, but we purchased them.

On the day of the track meet, I was the only student brave enough to run the 440 against Keith Sacket and Burt Swails. Keith had set a new college record in the mile the year before, and Burt had won the 440 the same year.

The race started. I shot off like a bullet. No one had told me how to run the race. I was still in the lead when we started the home stretch. I kept wondering, "When are they going to pass me?"

I kept looking back to see where they were. They were close but not closing. I thought, maybe I can win this race.

I won it by about four feet. The freshmen class treated me like a hero, for we were now ahead in the class competition.

The next race for me was the 220-yard dash. There were six runners at the start. The track was narrow. At the start, the runner on my left, Oliver Karkar, fell against me, and we both landed on our backs.

I got up and ran. I passed the first, then the second runner. I passed third runner on the curve. On the final stretch, there was one man ahead of me. I passed him about three feet from the finish.

Wow! I was a hero again.

The next race was the high hurdles. My brother Glenn and I were both in this race. I gave the track shoes to my brother, for it was his turn to wear them. I was going to run in tennis shoes.

Our father, observing this exchange, came over to us and said words that haunt me to this day. They were "Glenn, give the track shoes to Gordon, you don't have a chance."

I can still see the look on Glenn's face. It was complete rejection.

We had a great father. I am sure that he regrets using those words.

I lost the hurdles race, but that day, I was the anchor on the relay team that set the relay record for Houghton College. That record for that track remains today.

God Made Lemonade from a Lemon

It was October 1942, and I was a student at Houghton College (upstate New York). My first sexual encounter was with a fellow student, Grace, who happened to be the daughter of a missionary. She was my sister Lucille's best friend.

Grace got pregnant, and her father asked me to marry her. In those times, it was the only honorable thing to do. Being the person I was and not a real Christian, I lied and denied that I even touched her. Out of shame and to save the family from scorn and ridicule, she left Houghton College for the West Coast and had a baby daughter. Since single motherhood was unheard of back then, Grace had her daughter adopted by a loving family.

Throughout my life, the guilt and that familiar small voice tugged at my heart as I thought about this illegitimate daughter I had fathered in my self-centered youth. Before I married my current wife, Elida (May 1978), I told her that I had another daughter somewhere and that I had been searching for her.

A few months after my second marriage, we received an early morning phone call (2:00 AM). "We have found her," my sister Lucille said and provided me with Grace's address.

However, because of legal and privacy restrictions, she could not give us the address of my daughter, whom we found out later to be named Karen.

I sent a half-hour cassette tape to the mother, Grace, telling her about my life (the good, the bad, and the ugly). Grace, who forgave me and identified with many of my experiences, responded with a letter describing her life and revealed that she too had suffered the suicide of a child, and she sent my cassette to Karen.

Karen then sent me a twelve-page letter thanking me for causing her to be born. Thank God, abortion was not an easy option back in those days, especially for people who were deeply immersed in Christian beliefs.

Karen proceeded to send photos of her children and grandchildren. Wow, was I amazed! She had made me a great-grandfather. She confided to me about how she had found Jesus Christ as her personal Savior and she wanted to know if her birth parents knew Him too. What a blessing for all of us.

Elida and I have twice visited Karen in Everett, Washington. The first occasion, we took Karen to a large department store and lavished her with gifts and dressed her from head to toe. To relieve my guilt and make peace with that little nagging voice, I sought to compensate just a little for all of the birthdays and Christmases we missed being together.

We invited her to the Barnett family reunion in Houghton in 1992, where she met seventy-five additional family members and discovered her true ancestral roots. I introduced her to my entire family with these words, "This is my daughter, Karen. She loves me, and I never earned that love. She respects me and I never deserved that respect. She is heir to one quarter of my estate."

While at the reunion Karen got to know her new aunts, uncles, cousins, and two new brothers, Dennis and Doug, There was no doubt she was a Barnett with her prominent nose so common among many of the Barnett clan. They took the boat tour of Niagara Falls, and she felt comfortable with her newly discovered family.

The last time Elida and I visited her, she and I went for a walk. She told me that she was going to tell me something and I probably wouldn't like her anymore. I told her that nothing could change the love I had and the way I felt about her. She then admitted, "I am an alcoholic." I told her that I had given the disease to her and that I loved her just the same as God has loved me and helped me get sober. We shared some of our stories and compared dates of sobriety.

Karen is another gift of my mom's prayers, God's grace, and one of the many joys of my life. Our Jesus took a lemon and made sweet and delicious lemonade. My mother's prayers continued to cover and follow me.

Chapter 2

From December 8, 1942, to October 31, 1963

My First Navy Dentist

It was during May of 1943. I was in the Navy preflight training program at Del Monte, California, near Monterey. I had a cavity in a tooth, and they sent me to the dentist.

Without any Novocain, he started drilling on my tooth and kept the drill going until he felt that the cavity was ready for the filling. I cried out, "Ouch!"

The dentist said, "One more word out of you, cadet, and I will put you on report." When he squirted water on the tooth, steam came out of my mouth.

I never wanted to go to a Navy dentist again, but the time came when I had to. All of the rest of them were great, and my fears were unfounded.

I wonder how that dentist kept any customers when he went into civilian life.

I Cheated and Got Caught

It was in November 1943. I was in primary flight training at the Naval air station at Hutchison, Kansas.

A close friend and fellow Naval cadet, another Pastor's son, Jim Demmette, asked me to help him in a swimming test. He was supposed to tow me in the water for fifty meters. That was his last exercise in order to complete the program.

When we entered the pool area, he said, "Gordon, I want you to tow me instead of me towing you. You give your name as Demmette, and I will give mine as Barnett."

I knew the ruse was wrong, but I also I knew that I wanted to help my friend. It was pretty well established that he would wash out if he didn't pass this test. So I went along with the deception. I successfully towed him the fifty meters as required, but he took the credit as the "rescuer" and passed the swimming program.

Afterward, we dressed and were leaving the pool area when someone asked us to go to the pool officer in charge. Again, they asked us our names, and we lied as before.

When pressed, we finally broke down and revealed the deception. We were ordered to return to our barracks. We knew that we were going to be washed out and would have to spend the rest of our Navy careers on destroyers.

On the way, we were approached by the base Chaplain who coincidentally happened by and could see the worry and dejection in our demeanor.

He guessed something was wrong and asked what the problem was. We were quite ashamed but eventually admitted to him how we had cheated. He told us to continue on to our barracks and to pray for forgiveness.

Immediately, the Chaplain went to the base Commander and told him that he had been asked to vouch for cadets in the past and he refused because he didn't know them personally.

He told the Commander that there were two cadets with charges of cheating. He said, "I know these cadets. They attend chapel weekly. They are in the chapel choir. I implore that you give them a second chance."

The base Commander did as the Chaplain asked, but Jim Demmette would still have to pass the entire contingent of the swimming tests in one day. If he passed them all, we would be exonerated from all charges.

Jim confided in me that someone had previously passed nearly all of the other tests for him and he was afraid that he could not accomplish them on his own.

On being informed of this, I was shocked and terrified, for I knew that my career as a Naval aviator was in dire jeopardy.

I went back to the pool with Jim to give him moral support. However, the other participants were mad at us for all the trouble we had caused and wouldn't let me enter the pool area. So I stayed outside and prayed for Jim, in whom by this time I had little faith. It was probably the first time that I had petitioned the Lord in prayer in several months.

Miraculously, Jim passed the one-mile swim with clothes on. He passed the half-mile swim with clothes off. Then, he passed the underwater swim of fifty meters. Jim told me later that he struggled along the bottom by clawing the pool tiles.

And, last but not least, he passed the fifty-meter rescue-tow. The pool officer grabbed the first bystander he could find and ordered him to be the person hauled. This random sailor happened to be quite heavy and floated as Jim towed him the required fifty meters.

Jim emerged from the pool area with a grin that spoke volumes. He was so weak that he could hardly walk to our barracks, but his delight was palpable.

When we went to chapel the next Sunday, we praised the Lord by singing real loud in the choir and even put a generous offering in the plate with selfless joy and gratitude. Here again, my mother's prayers continued to cover and follow me.

Marvin Barnett

It was Saturday, October 1944, in Mobile, Alabama. John Bradley and I were walking down Main Street in our Naval cadet uniforms. We had hitchhiked from Barin Field, Alabama, for the weekend. A beautiful girl in a Cadillac convertible stopped and inquired, "How would you two cadets like to attend a champagne party this afternoon?" We both responded in the affirmative without hesitation. She then said, "Meet me at this same spot at 2:00 PM. Gordon, you will be my date. I will get another girl for your friend."

They took us to the party at the Mobile Country Club. Great food was in abundance and champagne was flowing, but champagne was not our style at that time.

Toward the end of the party, my date called her boyfriend back at Pensacola and said, "I am with a cute Naval cadet named Gordon Barnett." Her boyfriend was a Marine first lieutenant who just so happened to be my fighter pilot training instructor. When she told me about the phone call, I was worried because John and I were supposed to get our wings and commission within two weeks.

To add to my concern was the fact that I was the only cadet in our flight that had "killed" this same Marine flight instructor in an aerial fighter training dogfight. Actually, I "killed" him by accident. You see, he was on my tail about to shoot me down when I accidentally pulled up and stalled my aircraft and went into a spin. When I recovered from this maneuver, I was now on his tail. It is no wonder he was somewhat embarrassed by this incident.

In this fighter pilot training, we made gunnery runs at a long nylon sleeve towed by one of the cadets. The sleeve was towed one thousand yards behind the tow plane. Each of us had different-colored .30-caliber bullets. At the end of the day, they would count the number of our hits. We had to meet the required amount in order to successfully complete this phase of our training.

I was having lunch with a Cadet Foy back at Barin Field. He had the first tow of that morning. His sleeve got caught in the trees at the end of the runway, causing his aircraft to stall and crash in the trees. When Cadet Foy escaped from the aircraft, his parachute opened, so he carried it around the perimeter of the base to enter the main gate.

In the meantime, the fire crew had cut through the base fence and was looking for the "doomed pilot" of the downed aircraft.

Ironically, the Marines at the main gate would not let Cadet Foy enter the base because he had no ID card. It was like a scene from a comedy of errors: firemen searching for Cadet Foy and the Marines holding him at the gate.

Since I was scheduled to pilot the tow aircraft at 1300 hours that same day, I asked Foy what I could do to avoid having a similar predicament.

He told me to get the tail of my aircraft off the end of the runway so as to have maximum airstrip ahead, listen carefully to the engine at full throttle to rapidly get the aircraft in the air, and then climb just above stall speed to obtain as much altitude as possible.

Takeoff time arrived; I intended to follow Cadet Foy's advice exactly as he stated. Everything was going as planned until I lowered my head so I could hear my engine at full throttle.

Someone, I will never guess who, must have pushed my stick forward one-half of an inch when I lowered my head, because suddenly, the aircraft was sitting on its nose with a ruined prop and engine.

At that time, the Navy had too many pilots and was washing many of them out for even minor offenses. Damaging an expensive aircraft was more than a minor offense.

Up to then, I had been a promising Naval cadet for twenty-two months, going through the proverbial "an officer and a gentleman" regime twenty-four hours every day. But now, I knew I had blown my chances and the end was near; my dream to become a Naval aviator was most likely over.

The aforementioned Marine instructor, who already was not on my good side, came running to my damaged plane and screamed, "Cadet, you are going to Great Lakes to become a sailor." In my heart, I knew what he said was most likely true, but something inside me answered back without even thinking, "You want to bet?"

He immediately ordered me to see the chief flight instructor. So I went right then and there, still dressed in my flight suit.

I clicked my heels and stood in the doorway of the chief flight instructor. He instructed me to enter. I stood at attention in front of his desk. I noticed a sign on his desk that displayed his name. It was Lt. Marvin Barnett. He asked me why I was there.

I answered back with a question, "Are you a Methodist preacher's son?" His reply was yes. I proceeded to tell him that I was too. We talked about our childhoods and about our fathers. I also divulged the fact that I played organ for the base Methodist Chaplain, who told me about a Lt. Marvin Barnett that I must meet someday.

It was time to confess to Lt. Barnett why I was there and about my "problem," the accident, and the damaged plane.

He asked if I was flying at the time of the accident.

I answered with all honesty, "No."

He then asked me, "Were you taxiing?"

Again, I truthfully said, "No, my brakes were locked."

Finally, he said that he didn't know how to technically describe the incident, a flying accident or a taxiing accident. So I was dismissed.

The next morning I was scheduled for the first flight. My mother's prayers continued to protect and follow me.

The serendipity didn't end there. During 1950, I was on the staff of the Navy mines school at Yorktown, Virginia. At that time, I was considered the Navy's expert in aerial mine warfare. One day, I checked out an SNJ (the T-6 Texan, a single-engine trainer aircraft) at the Naval air station at Norfolk, Virginia. I flew it to Washington, DC, to talk to my detailer about my next assignment. When I approached his door, I could see that he was Lieutenant Commander Marvin Barnett.

I addressed him with the same confidence as I had done six years earlier with the following statement, "I owe you $50,000."

He said, "Sit down and let's discuss it." I related the story about the accident and his fortuitous technicality that undoubtedly kept me in the Navy's flight program, but he did not remember any of it. He then proceeded to say that a two-star admiral had requested me by name to be on his staff. Of course, I accepted the opportunity without hesitation.

During my tour on that two-star admiral's staff, I received a call from an Atlantic Fleet wing Commander to assist him in setting up a training program for his entire Navy AD squadrons. Lo and behold, it was again Marvin Barnett, now promoted to Commander (CDR).

The top the story off, in the year 1955, I was attached to the Naval air station at Pensacola, Florida. I joined the speaking organization Toastmasters and told the aforementioned story about my small-world encounters with this recurring Marvin Barnett. I finished my speech by thanking the present Navy Captain Marvin Barnett, a fellow Toastmaster. I told him in front of at least twenty-five other Toastmasters, "Thank you for canceling my $50,000 debt of gratitude." Once again, my mother's prayers continued to cover and follow me.

Romance and Marriage

I received my Navy "wings of gold" October 31, 1944, at the Naval air station at Pensacola, Florida. I was so proud and immediately took a train to Buffalo to display them and be with my family. My father met me at the train station and drove me to our home in upstate New York, a small village named Houghton. Houghton was a college town.

Since most of the men were at war, I was the only man on campus in a uniform, which made me the center of attention. It made me a little cocksure, which usually helps in the romantic department. In those days, it was like being a movie star.

There was a certain extremely beautiful brown-haired girl that I noticed almost everywhere I went. My family operated Barnett's Pantry, the only ice cream and hamburger parlor on the campus, and as expected, I put on an apron and worked behind the fountain. While working at the Pantry, I noticed the striking brunette was a frequent patron. It wasn't long before I discovered that she was a good friend of my only sister, Lucille, and that her name was Phyllis.

I got the courage to ask her out and we dated. During this relationship, I took a train to Boston to see another girlfriend, an old flame named Phoebe. I wanted to find out if I had gotten Phoebe out of my system. Phoebe was not out of my mind though, and she begged me not marry Phyllis. I looked deep into my heart and decided to go back to Houghton and be with Phyllis.

We eloped and secretly tied the knot in Belmont, New York, on November 22, 1944. It was an easy date to remember.

After the elopement, I left for Pensacola, Florida, to pick up my belongings and continued on to the Naval air station at Fort Lauderdale where I was trained to fly the TBF Avenger torpedo aircraft.

Back at Houghton, Phyllis wore her wedding ring on a gold chain around her neck. She kept the secret for a few days, but eventually confided in her good friend, the dean of women. The dean had to uphold her duties and reluctantly expelled Phyllis from college, since getting married without the school's permission was against the rules. My bride didn't care, since she really wanted to be with me—a lucky and happy man I was, indeed.

We shared an apartment in Fort Lauderdale, Florida, with Ken and Dotty Barnes (the couple in the aforementioned "His Eyes Were Brown").

I must admit, Phyllis was a stunning beauty (model potential by today's standards) and a very intelligent, caring, well-adjusted, independent thinker. (Near the demise of our twenty-seven-year marriage, this critical nature, although usually an admirable trait, played a role in one of our irreconcilable differences.)

She is the mother of my four wonderful children: Dennis, David, Douglas, and Darla. David took his own life at age twenty-four after struggles with drugs, Vietnam military service, and mental illness.

My First Son, Dennis

I was an ensign stationed on Key West, Florida, when I received word that my wife, Phyllis, was close to delivery of our firstborn.

I caught a Navy plane ride to Washington, DC, and flew commercial to Michigan where she was. I arrived there when my son was one day old.

When I arrived at her bedside, she said, "Gordon, he is ugly."

I then went to the nursery and viewed the babies through the glass. I looked at my son Dennis. He had red blotches on his forehead. His skin was gray. He had fuzz all over his head. His head came to a point like Denny Dimwit, a cartoon character. My wife was right; he was ugly.

Then another new father came alongside me to look at his child. His mother was with him. When they looked at my son, they started to laugh.

I was wearing my uniform. I stuck out my chest and bragged, "That is my son!"

They were embarrassed and they tried to make amends with statements like, "He is so cute."

It took only a few months for all the facial problems to go away, and his head rounded out to the normal look. Today he is a handsome man. He has been an ideal son. He is a missionary today to foreign students at the University of Minnesota in Minneapolis, Minnesota.

My Son Doug: Throw Him in the River

It was October 21, 1948. I was a student at the Navy's line school at Newport, Rhode Island. My wife, Phyllis, had labor pains that were very close. I took her to the Naval hospital, which was on the Naval base.

Her doctor told me that the baby would not come for a few hours and that I should go back to my last class for the day and return after class.

I returned to the hospital, and as I entered, I heard two Navy corpsmen talking about a LTJG's wife who wanted to throw her baby boy in the river.

I entered the ward of new mothers. When Phyllis saw me, she pointed at me and said while crying, "My next baby will be a test tube baby because you don't have any girls in you." Baby Douglas was our third baby boy. She was experiencing the aftereffects of some drug given during birth. She never remembered those words.

We were blessed with baby Darla Joyce Barnett three years later. She was not a test-tube baby. We rejoiced together.

Douglas Whitney Barnett has thanked us many times for not *throwing him in the river*. He and his wife, Lisa, visited Switzerland with us, and we enjoyed one another's company during May 2007 and visited Spain during May 2008.

Doug, who graduated with high honors from high school and college (and after getting clean and sober in 1984), is now a successful engineer and has been married to his loving Chinese wife, Lisa, since 2004.

My Daughter, Darla

When Darla was four years old, I was swinging her in our swings. She asked me to push her higher, then higher and higher. At the top, she fell out of the swing and landed on her head. She was unconscious.

I took her to the hospital. They x-rayed her and checked her over and found nothing wrong with her.

Just before she died from pancreatic cancer on February 19, 1997, she and I went for a walk. I told her about this accident and begged her forgiveness for hurting her on the swings.

She then told me, "Dad, I thought that I could fly. I tried it twice and failed both times."

Darla died tragically at age forty-five, survived by my two fantastic grandchildren, Cy and Jessica.

Duty in Virginia

During 1950, the Commander Fleet Air Wings, Atlantic, a two-star admiral, requested that I be transferred to his staff to initiate and train all patrol aircraft in the Atlantic in the art of aerial mine warfare.

While on this staff, the Commander Carrier Attack, Atlantic Fleet, had me organize an aerial mine warfare training program for his and all other attack squadrons. His name was CDR. Marvin E. Barnett, a Methodist preacher's kid who had saved my flying carrier in Pensacola many years before. That great story I have related earlier in this chapter.

While on his staff, the aforementioned admiral sent me to Hawaii to help the Navy design a jet seaplane minelayer. It was designated as the P6M. It crashed during testing, and it was dropped from the aircraft program. A friend of mine, Phil Fisher, was killed in the crash.

Duty in Panama

Thereafter, the Navy sent me to Panama to learn to fly the PBM and to become a patrol plane Commander (PPC). This designation is necessary to be the commanding officer (CO) of any VP aircraft squadron. At that time, I was a novice two-striper, or a full LT (lieutenant).

Ironically, while stationed in Panama for those eleven months, my present wife-to-be, Elida was just ten miles away on the other side of Panama. She was only three years old. I don't think I would have whistled at her at that time like I do now.

Life in Pensacola During 1953 to 1956

I was transferred from Panama to Pensacola, Florida, in December 1953. My children were ages seven, six, five, and two. What a glorious time of my life!

Buzz Borries was the executive officer (XO) of NAS Pensacola. He had requested that I be transferred there. I had worked directly for him on a two-star admiral's staff in Norfolk before going to Panama.

Commander Borries had three Navy lieutenants that he considered his firemen. If any area on the base had a problem, he assigned one of the lieutenants to that area to fix it. With me, he continued to give me jobs until I had eighteen of them. He never took any of them away from me.

One of the jobs was officer in charge and treasurer of the nursery and kindergarten. I had a staff of twenty-four ladies. I gave them one bit of advice and that was whenever a parent came to pick of a child that the parent was to be told one thing that the child had done that day.

We charged twenty-five cents per hour for the first and second child, and the rest of the children in this family would be free for officers. For enlisted, it was twenty cents as above. Our profits exceeded the profits of the officers' club every month.

We made so much money that we spent $100,000 to build another building. We had graduation ceremonies for five-year-olds as they graduated into the public school's kindergarten. We had the mothers make caps and gowns out of sheets.

A US congressman from that area wrote to the CO of NAS Pensacola that we were hurting the local public nurseries. It was an easy letter to answer.

Another job that I was given was senior member of a civil service discipline and advisory committee. We heard cases and recommended punishment of civil service people, even to being fired.

One particular case was the case of Charley Tate. He had closed down an assembly line in aircraft O&R. Another committee tried to hear his case, but he wouldn't talk to them, because they were lily-white. The CO of the base asked me if I thought that I could handle it. I agreed that I could. When his case started, he tried the same lily-white story.

I told Charley Tate, "The representative of the civil service here today is a Jew." If he used the same analogy, he would be discriminating against us. I then pointed out two representatives in the back who were from the NAACP. I had asked them to be there to verify if the hearings were fair. I told him that we were going to hold the hearings today, and if he did not present his case, we would recommend that he be fired. He said that he would talk.

He had closed down the assembly line because he thought that they had taken out too much for taxes in his last paycheck and he wanted to go to get a loan. He had done this two times before. He was fired.

Sitting in on this case was CDR. Buck Hoer, the representative from the Pensacola overhaul and repair department, the one who recommended that Mr. Tate be fired.

A few years later, during 1959, Capt. Buck Hoer was on the selection board that selected me for promotion to Commander. At the time when only 33 percent of the lieutenant Commanders would be selected, I was in the WWII hump of excess officers. Again, my mother's prayers covered me, for I was selected.

Our Aircraft Crashed

It was during the spring of 1955. A Marine major was flying a T-28 from Pensacola to James Connally AFB near Waco, Texas. My brother Bob was stationed there. I went along as a passenger. I had never flown the T-28. Before departure, I read the emergency procedures for the aircraft just in case there was a problem.

Our flight was uneventful as we cruised at eleven thousand feet. We started taking on ice, especially on all our antennas. They lowered us to eight thousand feet.

When we passed over College Station, Texas, a red light came on in the back cockpit. I called this to the major's attention. He relayed back to me that we had two hundred pounds (thirty-three gallons) of fuel left. I thought that he said two hundred gallons.

We continued on in the soup. They held us over Dallas for forty-five minutes and then cleared us to Waco with a low-frequency range approach to the AFB.

We crossed low-cone and headed for the base, when the most intense silence that I ever heard, happened. The engine was silent. We were out of fuel.

I called the tower and told them that we were out of fuel, were eight miles from the field, and we were going to land wheels up, cross-grained to the furrows in a large cotton field.

When they heard me say that we were going to land wheels up, the major put the wheels down. Never are you to land wheels down, except on a runway.

We heard the staccato of the wheels touching the tops of the cotton furrows. We plowed through 113 yards of mud, the nose wheel broke, the nose dove into the mud, our aircraft started to flip over on its back. It didn't. We settled on our main mounts in a forty-five-degree nose-down attitude.

We had only plastic over our heads. Never has a pilot survived a T-28 that flipped over on its back.

My first remarks were "Who signed for this aircraft?" The major made a statement that I can't express in this story.

Back at the operations building, my brothers Bob and David were waiting when they heard the announcement "Navy aircraft has crashed." David, a civilian, said to Bob, the USAF first lieutenant, "Bob, do something."

Bob asked, "What do you want me to do?"

We were fine. The Marine had to do much explaining why he lowered the wheels.

My mother's prayers continued to cover me.

John Wayne and Gordon Barnett

During 1956, I was a movie star. John Wayne and other movie stars came to Pensacola to make part of the movie "The Wings of Eagles".

I was watching the filming when a man asked me if I was six feet tall. I told him that I was. He said that they needed an extra that was six feet tall because John Wayne was so tall.

John would bum cigarettes from me because he never carried them. I would give him a Pall Mall. He then bawled me out for giving him a cigarette with a filter. He would tear off the filter and smoke the cigarette.

Wayne was the kindest of men. He would take a child from its mother, hold it, and ask the mother to take a picture. Dan Dailey was a grouch.

Maureen O'Hara was the sweetest lady. One day, just before Maureen was to go in front of the klieg lights, she closed her eyes and looked up toward the sun for about a minute. She would then go into the scene. I asked her why she did that. She said that she didn't know, but an old star had told her to do it many years ago. I then told her that when she did that, her pupils would shrink very small and that she would not blink when she went in front of the bright lights. She told me that no one had ever told her that before.

Every noon, they took us the beach on the base and fed us from a chuck wagon. I ate lunch daily with Festus from *Gunsmoke*. The food was scrumptious.

I was in many scenes during the filming. I was only in one scene in the finished picture. It was the scene when John Wayne was going to take off in a small seaplane to show an Army Major that he was a great pilot. Wayne was not qualified to fly at that time.

Maureen O'Hara ran down a ramp into the water yelling for him to stop. At the time, I led a group of flight cadets toward some oil drums yelling for him to stop. He took off anyway.

During his flight, he made a diving pass on a train going over a trestle. A man on the top of the train dove from the train into the water. The boat scheduled to pick the man out of the water was late, and the man almost drowned.

Wayne flew through a hangar at the Pensacola Municipal Airport as scheduled. The aircraft dragged its skid on the deck of the hangar as it went through. A stunt pilot was really doing the flying.

Since I was on active duty and could not receive pay for this activity, I expected none, but a week after they left town, a blank envelope appeared in my mailbox that contained four ten-dollar bills. I had worked four days. I kept the money.

Noel Bacon

During the year 1948, I was a student at the Navy General Line School at Newport, Rhode Island. In our class of thirty Naval officers was a LCDR. Noel Bacon. He had been a Flying Tiger with General Chennault during the war in China. They were fighting against the Chinese communists under General Chiang Kai-shek.

Later, during 1955, CDR. Noel Bacon was the XO of the aircraft Carrier home ported at Pensacola. It was used in the training of Naval aviators for Carrier landings.

A hurricane had struck Nicaragua and the Carrier was being sent to that country loaded with helicopters and other needs.

I was the assistant to the XO of Pensacola. The CO was on the golf course, the XO was off the base when I received a call from Noel Bacon from the Carrier.

He said, "The Carrier needed fifty thousand rounds of 50-caliber ammunition before it could depart. I have sent my ammunition people to your depot on the base, and the LCDR in charge would not issue it because we had the wrong form and there were no correct forms available."

I told Noel to send his ammunition people back, and they would deliver it this time.

I then called the LCDR, our ammunition officer, and told him to issue it without the correct form. I was a lieutenant talking to a lieutenant Commander. He said that he would. That he did.

During 1959, when I was selected for Commander, Capt. Noel Bacon was on my selection board. My mother's prayers continued to follow me.

A Lump, Not a Hole

Another one of these eighteen jobs while stationed at Pensacola was the prosecutor (trial counsel) in special courts-martial. I won my first 105 cases, which resulted in putting 105 men in prison. I soon became disillusioned with this position. In today's Navy, one now has to be a qualified lawyer to do that what I had to do back then.

So I requested to become a defense counsel. On my first case, I defended a sailor who was charged with altering his ID card to purchase liquor. My friend, Casey Campbell, another lieutenant, was the prosecutor on the case.

Earlier in our careers, I flew with Casey to my brother Bob's wedding in Bradford, Pennsylvania. During the trail, when Casey had the shore patrol witness testify that there was a hole in the ID card, the accused leaned over and whispered in my ear, "It's not a hole, it's a lump." I informed my client (the accused defendant) to be silent.

When Casey's witness (the shore patrol sailor) had finished his testimony, I began my cross-examination. I walked over to the witness box, took the witness' sailor's cap and concealed the ID with his hat, and left it on the railing of the witness box.

I then had the witness tell the court three times that there was a hole in the ID card.

I then walked to the back of the courtroom and asked the witness to lift up his hat. I asked, "Is that the altered ID card in question?"

He answered, "Yes, it is."

I then asked him to get up out of the witness box and take the ID card and show the hole to each member of the court (military jury).

The witness immediately exclaimed, "It is not a hole, it is a lump."

The defendant was acquitted, and Casey Campbell harbored resentment toward me for at least three hours. However, he knew that I, as a defense attorney, must do everything within my power to win the case for the accused. Actually, I didn't really win, Casey lost it. He had not properly done his homework that time.

Duty in Hawaii

After my stint in Pensacola, I was transferred to Hawaii to be on the staff of a four-star admiral, the Commander in chief of the US Pacific Fleet. My new position was that of Manpower Utilization Officer.

This included oversight of all the ships and shore stations in the Pacific Fleet. My task was to properly utilize all manpower in the fleet. Everybody wanted more people, more spaces, and more billets. Congress had allocated the limits, and we had to function within them. At this stage in my Navy career, I was a recently promoted LCDR. My job required me to travel throughout the Pacific and inspect many ships and shore stations.

Mrs. Carpenter, a Most Remarkable Woman

Early in 1957, I was attached to the staff of the Commander of the Pacific Fleet in Oahu, Hawaii.

Shortly after my arrival, my wife and I attended a cocktail party.

When we arrived at the party, we noticed that most of the women were in one part of the room. In another part of the room was a huddle of the men surrounding one particular and remarkable woman.

I sent my wife to the women's circle, and I joined the huddle of men. As I approached the group, the lady in the center, knowing I was a newcomer, drew me into the gathering and introduced me to all the rest. It gave me an immediate sense of acceptance.

This lady, Mrs. Carpenter, wasn't an exceptionally attractive woman. But she had a unique characteristic of only talking about the others around her and not herself. She was the complete antithesis of the self-centered woman. Shortly after she introduced me to everyone at the party, she became, in my eyes, a most beautiful and attractive woman.

Her outgoing nature and self-effacing humility made all the men want to be in her presence. And contrary to what you'd expect, the other women also loved to be around her. I learned an important lesson that day—to take the focus off oneself. From that day on, I wanted to pattern my life after hers.

After working in this capacity for about two years, I was transferred to a patrol squadron at Barbers Point, Hawaii.

When I reported in to Patrol Squadron 28, I told John Trautman, the CO, "I guarantee that we will win the Navy's coveted E."

He asked why I was so sure, and I told him that every patrol squadron that I had been in had won this award. He just smiled. One year later, he had a bigger smile after VP-28 was given Navy battle efficiency "E" award.

One way this was accomplished was that in VP-28, my crew, crew number 7, challenged the other eleven crews in every operation that we performed. That competitive spirit grew and flourished, and it made the job fun as well as successful.

While in VP-28, my promotion zone was going through selection for CDR. The Navy was in the worst of the WWII hump, or surplus of officers, and only one out of three candidates was to be selected. Of those who were selected among the aviators, only one in six would ever obtain a command of a squadron.

I had a lot of factors going against me. Keep in mind, I was only a high school graduate (I left college to join the Navy before graduating), I never had sea duty as a shipboard officer, and I was not a Naval Academy graduate.

In my favor, though, I had several very good report cards (performance records and achievements). And I had been attending night school at the University of Hawaii working toward my BA.

Then, and most importantly, there were my mother's prayers following me throughout my lifetime.

It was an early 2:00 AM when I received a call one morning from that four-star staff duty officer (the one I had left about a year prior). The officer said to me, "Gordon, you're on the team, you made it!" Even with all the things going against me, I felt in my gut that I would make it. At that time, I took credit for all my successes, not realizing that God and my mother's prayers were placing the hand of the Lord on my life's journey.

In VP-28, we already had two Commanders as CO and XO. To make matters worse, all three of us who were LCDRs were selected for CDR. There was a reconnaissance squadron across the hangar that had fifty-four LCDRs in the zone, and only four of them made the cut.

Due to this top-heavy competitive situation, I sent a message to the Bureau of Naval Personnel in Washington that basically stated that five (5) Commanders in VP-28 was excessive and requested to be removed immediately.

The bureau consented and sent me to a squadron in San Diego (VP-31) to be the XO. This Southern California squadron (located in beautiful North Island, Coronado) trained all pilots and air crewmen sent to other VPs throughout the Pacific. To further indicate the Lord's providence in my career and the professional success of this unit, three (3) of the lieutenants who served under me in VP-31 later became admirals.

Escape and Evasion / Survival

During the year 1959, I was attached to VP-28, a Pacific Fleet patrol squadron. It was home ported at Barbers Point NAS, Hawaii. We were deploying to Japan after training. All pilots and aircrews were required to go through escape and evasion survival training prior to deployment. This training was required since the Korean War.

My class consisted of four officers and twenty-six enlisted sailors. I was a LCDR and was the senior officer. Two of the sailors were from my squadron. The other officers and sailors were from other squadrons.

We had about one week of school prior our training in the field. The training in the field was similar to wartime experiences. It was real in our minds.

We were to cross miles of the Hawaiian jungle and were to arrive at a certain point days later. US Marines outfitted as Russian communist soldiers were to impede our travel. We were given a hunting knife, one canteen of water, and no food. We must find water and food on our way.

I held brainstorming sessions with all the first night. I told them that if we were captured, if anyone was offered anything by the enemy, he was to take it and give it to another person in our group. No one was to keep anything that was given to them. He was to take it and give it to another.

During that first night, we found that we had a water thief among us. I held an immediate meeting and authorized them to first strike with their knife if their canteen of water was touched by anyone. I told them that I would defend them in any court-martial if they were charged for attacking the water thief.

One morning after a rain, I drank from the top of a mud puddle with my face in the water. The cleanest water was on the top. It tasted good because my thirst was beyond description.

The first day, my stomach hurt, but from then on, it felt comfortable. My thirst for water was agonizing. We found a guava tree that had some fruit on it. The guava tasted delicious. They supplied food and liquid.

We had to hide many times because of the presence of the enemy.

Finally, we arrived at our destination and were to spend the night on the ground. That night an aircraft dropped C rations to us. The food tasted great, but I was sorry that I ate it because we had no water. The food made me thirstier. During the night, the enemy bothered us and would not let us sleep.

The next morning, we all were captured as required in our training.

We were taken to a large cave in a large hill. Since I was the senior officer, I was put in a hole in the ground; it was like a shallow grave. It was so shallow that I could not sit up. They covered the hole with a heavy piece of iron about one-half inch thick. An enemy soldier would strike the iron with the butt of a rifle, and it would ring like a bell. I sang old hymns that I remembered from my childhood. My ears hurt.

They were marching the rest of our crew in the hot sun just outside the cave. Finally, they brought all of my troops into the cave and had them standing at close intervals.

They brought me out of the hole and handed me an aluminum cup filled with ice water and told me that all of them had drunk all that they wanted and wanted me to drink the rest. The aluminum cup was sweating with water drops on its outside.

I was dying of thirst and I know they my crew had had no water. I took the cup. I stood between the man who had offered me the water and the first of my men in line. He was from my aircraft crew.

I gave the cup to this man and said, "Drink it fast!" He did. They struck me and then put me back in the hole.

One of my men was ordered to work for the enemy. He was to make coffee and do other jobs for their comfort. He started to work and then quit. He told them that he would work no more for them. They put him back in the group that they were punishing.

I lost twenty pounds of body weight during this training. I don't recommend this as a steady diet.

Finally, the enemy gave up. They could not get any of the officers or enlisted men to break down or sign a confession.

The officer in charge of the enemy wrote a letter to my squadron commanding officer stating that this was the only class ever with which they were unable to get at least one man to break down or confess. I was given credit for this inaction.

That was the last recommendation put in my Navy record before my selection for Commander. Only one in three of the lieutenant Commanders were selected for Commander.

My mother's prayers continued to follow me.

It Is Better to Climb the Mountain

I was the plane Commander in a Navy P2V-5. The plane had two recips, or reciprocating engines, and two jets. It was a typical tropical Hawaiian February (1959) when the flight began. We were on a three-leg navigation expedition. One of the legs took us close to the 10,023-foot Mount Haleakala (Maui, Hawaii). After four hours into the flight, many clouds gathered, and we were soaring into an obscured soup.

For some undefined reason, I felt uneasy, and admittedly, I was worried. Then I heard a small voice say, "Go back and check the navigation." We already had a navigator on duty, and it would be insulting for me to question his competence, but something nagged at me to go back and check anyway.

I quickly obtained a three-line loran fax and plotted it and ordered my copilot to do a 180-degree hard right turn. My unhesitating gut reaction was well founded. We were fatally heading for a point five hundred feet below the top of Mount Haleakala.

At that time, I was not a committed follower of Jesus Christ, but I wondered if this small voice was from Him. Again, the serendipities of a maternal petition were taking a ubiquitous role in my life. Yep, my mother's prayers continue to cover and follow me.

Duty on NAS North Island, San Diego, California: My Sword Stabs a Hat

It was a comfortable winter, January 1962. I was stationed in San Diego, California, at NAS North Island as the XO of VP-31, a Pacific Fleet antisubmarine training squadron. CDR. George Koenig, the CO, was a stickler for military pomp and ceremony. He required us to pass and review with swords during a Friday's "routine" inspection. Imagine the logistics of eight hundred officers and men passing in review, eight abreast.

I had mustered the squadron at quarters, and we were prepared for inspection when CDR. George Koenig arrived. I saluted him with the customary sword salute. As I was about to raise my sword to the forward-and-upward position, the tip caught the rim of my hat, lifting it off my head into the air.

What a sight it was! There I stood at attention, saluting my commanding officer with my hat on the tip of my sword.

The quandary was how to get it down and back on my head in the proper ceremonious military fashion expected by CDR. George Koenig. In short, there was no way.

Everybody held back as long as possible, but finally busted out in laughter.

Without missing a beat, I took the hat off the sword and placed it on my head. Being a good sport and realizing the humor of the somewhat unavoidable accident, George Koenig told the squadron artist to draw a caricature of the scene.

Duty on Okinawa: I Woke Up President Kennedy

It was in December 1962. I was the commanding officer of VP-4. We were home ported at Naha, Okinawa. My crew in YD-1 was on a track through the Taiwan Strait, with Jim Taylor as the patrol plane Commander. We at squadron headquarters received a message from Jim that they had sighted a Russian submarine. My operations officer, Art Schlofman, prepared a message for me to sign. It was to notify many of the defense intelligence agencies about this sighting.

When Art typed the message, one of the pages in the top secret book flipped over, and he typed the code group that said we had sunk a Russian submarine.

I checked the code group and then signed the message. It went out to the world.

Shortly thereafter, I received a phone call from an admiral in Hawaii on CINCPACFLT staff. He asked in plain language, "Gordon, do you mean that we are at war?" I said no.

He said, "Send your message again. I will call Washington to let them know things are OK."

I found out later that President Kennedy got out of bed and did go back to bed when he found out about the second message.

I waited to be relieved of my command, but it did not come. The senior officer in Hawaii knew my reputation. He did ask for recommendations so that it would not happen again. My recommendations were implemented. Again, my mother's prayers followed me.

My Praying Mother, Lucy Minerva Barnett

My first flight in the Navy

The Neptune, P2V-7, the aircraft that we flew in
VP-4

My last flight in the Navy

Chapter 3

From October 31, 1963, to the Present

Government Personnel Mutual Life Insurance Company

The year was 1963. I had just retired from the US Navy. I had sent my resume to over one hundred companies and had little response. I had interviewed with two companies with no positive results.

Finally, I received a response from the Government Personnel Mutual Life Insurance Company. They gave me many tests, and then they offered me $1,000 per month to start selling life insurance.

The following day, I received a phone call from a Prudential Life Insurance agent trying to sell me some life insurance.

I thought that I could get rid of him by telling him that I was going to work for the Government Personnel Mutual Life Insurance Company. He turned me over to his Division Leader, who asked me the name of the company that I was going to work for.

I said to him, "Government Personnel Mutual Life Insurance Company."

He asked me, "Tell me that name again?"

I said, "Government Personnel Mutual Life Insurance Company."

He said, "Please tell me again?"

I said, "Government Personnel Mutual Life Insurance Company."

Finally, he said, "Wouldn't you rather say The Prudential?"

I agreed and went to work for The Prudential. They offered me nothing. I had to earn to get paid.

I was their agent of the year shortly thereafter. I was a member of the Million Dollar Round Table for four years in a row; I was awarded the professional degree of CLU five years later.

Pepperdine University and My Master's Thesis

I received my master's degree at Pepperdine University in 1974. When I attended, Pepperdine University was in the Watts area, a sometimes turbulent inner-city district of Los Angeles, California. It has since moved to the more upscale Malibu.

I was one of only two whites in a class of twenty students. The rest were black.

In that class, I encountered two of the most prejudiced people that I have ever known, and they were black. The only reason they disliked me was that I was white. By the time of our graduation, we became good friends, and they didn't know why.

Perhaps, like all people with prejudices against general groups, once they get to know the individual, they realize that basically we are all the same, just imperfect people in an imperfect world with similar good and bad traits molded from the human condition.

Our final exam was to write a master's thesis. Mine was titled "Can Churches Integrate?"

Because of despondency from my middle son's recent suicide and the dissolution of my twenty-seven-year marriage, I enlisted the assistance of my youngest son, Doug, to help me with the thesis. Doug was an out-of-work college student who had recently graduated with high honors, pol-sci, prelaw with a minor in math, from San Diego State University.

My Pastor, Orval C. Butcher, asked that I write on the subject of the integration of blacks into the basically all-white Skyline Wesleyan Church, because blacks were moving into Lemon Grove, California, and he wanted to know how to make it work.

Before distributing the survey, the Pastor endorsed participation from the pulpit without complete knowledge of the survey's content. Needless to say, there was some controversy about the questionnaire's intent.

Certain questions were posed about white feelings concerning interracial dating and marriage and caused quite a stir. More than 67 percent of people responded to the survey (all were white), and the results were quite revealing. The average disapproval of interracial dating and marriage was nearly 70 percent. The older the respondent, the more disapproval.

The most revealing aspect of the survey was the many unsolicited handwritten comments on the back of the survey that attempted to explain the reasons (and rationalizations) for the respondent's answers. These I incorporated into the thesis to give it more than a dry statistical analysis. Ironically, although the majority of the church disapproved of interracial dating and marriage, 95 percent approved of allowing black attendance to their church.

One of my professors, a black man, gave me a B+ in a subject. The head of the department asked the grading professor why he only awarded a B+ to his best student. The professor replied to the dean, "I won't give an A to a white." I know this to be true because the dean told me so.

All of the rest of my grades were As. My final grade point was a 3.8. I harbor no ill feelings and was grateful for the B+.

Divorce

My marriage to Phyllis lasted twenty-seven years and ended not so amicably because of various reasons: David's mental illness and suicide, the new morality and high divorce rates of the early '70s, personality and irreconcilable differences, but mostly because of my alcohol-fueled erratic and abusive behavior. Now, by God's grace, the love of my forgiving Jesus, and the initial help of AA, I have been sober since January 18, 1984, and am now married to a wonderful woman, my sweet and devoted Elida. My sobriety, salvation, and second marriage I owe to my mother's prayers that continue to cover and follow me.

Alcohol

Alcohol became a very important part of my life. It hampered my million-dollar life insurance sales. It caused me to become a very poor husband and father. It ruined every good thing about my life.

Because of my erratic behavior mainly due to my alcoholism, my second son, David, took his own life in June 1973. He was twenty-five years old. He knew that his parents' marriage was falling apart. He had been on the drug scene for a few years.

David wrote a suicide note, put the barrel of a rifle in his mouth, pulled the trigger, and died. Soon after I buried my son, my wife divorced me and remarried.

In six months, my father died, my son died, my wife divorced me. My children were ashamed of me.

I had no friends.

I considered suicide.

I *was alone.*

I went to Spain to get away from my problems, but amazingly, my problems came right with me. I traveled by military space-available.

All the more, alcohol was welcomed into my life. I thought that alcohol could solve all my problems. I would start drinking at 5:00 AM and continue until the day disappeared.

I thought that alcohol could help me forget my pain, my pain, my pain. I left work, for you can't work drunk.

I went traveling around the world looking for something. I went completely around the world three times, and I still could not find what I was looking for. I did not know what I was looking for.

I rented a condo near the airport in Madrid. It was to be my home for fourteen years.

I Went to Spain

The Pueblo Cobeña, Spain

It was during the year of 1975; I visited friends who lived in Cobeña, Spain, quite often. The pueblo was behind the Torrejon AFB. The little pueblo planned a bullfight using the youth of Cobeña as bullfighters.

I went with the elders of the pueblo to purchase some bulls. They wanted them big enough to thrill the people, but small enough for the youth to fight. I watched as they selected the little bulls. The field was full of many large and a few small bulls. They told me that bulls get along peacefully together, but when you put one female cow in the field, a war starts.

They built a fenced bullring next to the large Catholic church.

On the day of the bullfight, the pueblo was a carnival. Games were played, with prizes given to the winners. One of the booths was run by two Spanish girls about fourteen years of age. Their father was watching the bulls, and the girls were running the booth alone. A man started taking their prizes without paying the price or playing the game.

A *guardia civil* (Spanish policeman) watched for a short time, and then he went to the thief, grabbed him, took him to the one jail cell in Cobeña. It was on the second floor of a building. He shoved the thief in, locked the door, and left.

The guardia civil came back the next morning and let him out. The jail had no toilet, no food, and no blankets.

In Franco's days, the guardia civil could be judge and jury without filling out one paper. They were respected and obeyed. If a man was sexually harming a little girl, they would shoot him on the spot with little paperwork to follow.

I always felt comfortable when they were around.

The Running of the Bulls in Pamplona

It was in the year 1976. I was living in Madrid. This was during my alcoholic days. I had read about the running of the bulls in Pamplona, and I thought that it might be fun to watch. They start at the seventh hour of the seventh day of the seventh month of the year. And they run for seven days in a row.

It took almost a half of a day driving to get there. I drove there on July 6, the day before the start. All of the hotels were full. The town was full of people. I had to sleep in my auto. The bathrooms in all of the bars and restaurants were a mess.

They released seven bulls and seven horned steers the morning of July 7. Their path led to the city bullring and was boarded at the cross streets. Every day, all of the bulls were fought and killed in the bullring.

Many men and boys ran ahead of the bulls. They had to be drunk to get the courage to run with the bulls. The bulls caught and passed many of the runners.

It appeared that the bulls injured many of the runners, but that day, none of the runners was injured. An observer was killed. He was an Australian man who was drunk. He had leaned out too far from a top balcony. He fell to the ground, landed on his head, and died.

One bonus, health care was free for anyone injured during the running.

Elida Enters My Life

From 1973 to 1978, I was a drunk living in Madrid Spain. I was a full-blown alcoholic. My days started at 5:00 AM, when I would take my first drink. I would continue to drink until the day disappeared. I must have enjoyed, for I did it every day.

In February 1978, I put a want ad in a newspaper in Madrid. It was the *Herald Tribune*. The ad was to meet more women. Elida thought that it was an ad for a job, and she sent me her CV. She had a tremendous job with a tremendous salary, but she answered my phony add. *Why?*

I made an appointment to interview her. I picked her up at her downtown Madrid address on February 11, 1978. We went to a café for breakfast. It was ten o'clock on a Saturday morning. She ordered a hot tea. I ordered a café con leche and a cognac. Mine was a great breakfast for a drunk.

I asked her one question, "What do you want out of life?" She thought that it was a stupid question for someone looking for a secretary. I wasn't looking for a secretary.

She answered, "I want to love and be loved." I thought that was a great answer. When she made that statement, she knew that I was the man whom she was going to marry. She was twenty-seven years old; I was double her age, fifty-four, and I was an alcoholic having a cognac for breakfast.

We just talked about our lives. During our interview, she had to call and cancel a luncheon date with an American man. She told him that she would be busy. He asked about the next day. She would be busy. He asked about next week. She would be busy. He finally hung up on her.

Thirty days later, on March 13, 1978, she proposed marriage to me. I said no. I told her I didn't trust women and "I have a daughter your age."

She answered, "I am not your daughter." Four days later, on March 17, 1978, I said yes. During those four days, I thought that I could trust her. I also thought, "When you get old, she can take care of you." *Guess what, we are there now.*

On May 2, 1978, we married in Gibraltar. At that time, a divorced person could not get married in Spain.

In Proverbs 22:6, it says, "Train a child in the way he should go, and when he is old, he will not depart from it."

Something within me gave me the *urge* to attend a Bible-believing church. They were starting a new mission in our area, so we went. It was all in Spanish. My wife understood it all. At that time, I didn't understand Spanish very well.

On September 15, 1978, at a Bible study in our home, we both committed our lives to Jesus Christ. It was my mother's eightieth birthday. She had prayed for me for five years, ten years, twenty years, thirty years, fifty-four years before her prayers were answered. I was the last of her eight children to make this commitment.

We phoned Mother that evening. More than $50 worth of tears on my phone bill were shed by both my mother and me, after she understood the good news that her prodigal had come home, that the last of her eight children had made that commitment.

We started reaching out to our neighbours. We lived in a nine-story condominium with four condos on each floor. Out of the thirty-six condos, five families either fully or partially came to our Jesus during our fourteen years living there.

I was unable to quit drinking. I became a closet drinker. Until I asked for help from the USAF Medical at Torrejon AFB close to Madrid, I was living a nonvictorious life. They gave me orders to the Navy base at Rota, Spain, for six weeks of alcohol rehabilitation treatment. They sent Elida through the same treatment to better assist me.

A Light in My Life

The Elida Line

During 1978, soon after we married, we were traveling in our Citroën from Madrid to Cordoba. Ron and Brenda Anderson, new missionaries in Spain, were with us. Elida was driving.

Elida had a cast on her right arm for I had broken her arm. A week before, she had hugged me while I was taking a siesta. This startled me, and I turned over quickly and broke her arm.

Elida was still working as the executive secretary to the director of Burger King Spain. Because of her broken arm, she was given a *baja*. This meant that she could not work, but her salary would continue.

We were traveling in the Spanish countryside among olive groves. The road was straight. We were going up a hill. There was one auto ahead of us. Elida passed the auto, but crossed over the double line before she could get back in her lane.

At the top of the hill was a guardia civil, a member of the gestapo in Spain. He stood in the highway and waved for us to stop.

All of the members in our auto could speak perfect Spanish; I was a beginner. They told me to exit our auto and speak to the cop and show him my Navy Commander ID card.

I spoke only in English. He understood none of it. I showed him my ID card. He was not impressed. He was frustrated with the whole ordeal.

He looked at Elida's arm in a cast. He told her to move over to the passenger's side and for me to drive. He waved us on.

Since that time, some of the missionaries in Spain call the double line "the Elida line."

She Gave Me Her Seat on the Bus

It was during the year 1988; I was taking a bus from downtown Madrid to our home near the airport. It was rush hour. I was standing, for the bus was packed.

Two Spanish girls about fifteen years of age who were sitting in seats next to me were talking. They looked at me. One of them got up and offered me her seat. I took it, and the girls kept talking.

I was then sixty-five years of age. How did they know that I was old?

Roland

Roland spoke with a German accent. Elida and I met him where he was a patient in a San Antonio Nursing Home. It was the year 1993. We had moved from Madrid Spain to San Antonio the year before.

We went to the Nursing Home Supervisor with the question, "Which of your patients have the fewest visitors?" From them, we selected two elderly ladies and two elderly men. We visited them weekly. Soon we were family.

One of them was a man named Roland.

Every time we visited Roland, he would tell us about his boyhood home in Connecticut on the Hudson River. He described all sections of the small town. He told us about the green grass just outside of the courthouse, the grocery stores, the filling stations, the town library and many paths down to the river. He continually said that he wanted to go back for another visit.

One Tuesday when we visited Roland, he was crying. It was unusual for he was such a stoic person. I asked him why the tears? He responded, "This morning my son visited me. When I told him that I wanted to visit my childhood home town once again, he told me that we could never do that for I was too old and too sick to go back."

Elida immediately told Roland, "Roland, when you can get out of that bed, Gordon and I will take you there." You should have seen the smile on his face.

Thereafter, we brought a map to this town and pinned them on the wall next to his bed. We continually discussed with him the routes that we would take going there.

I wonder what his son thought the next time he visited his dad.

Sometime later, I felt led to discuss Heaven and having Eternal Life, so I shared my 3 minute testimony about Forgiveness, Grace and my mother's praying for me for 54 years. At the end I used the 4 Spiritual Laws. He prayed to receive Christ.

When he finished, I asked Roland, "Did you really mean it? Were you sincere?"

Roland immediately responded in a loud voice, "You dam right, I meant it."

When we walked in Roland's room the next week, the bed was empty. We went to the supervisor and questioned about Roland.

She told us that he had died and that the funeral had been a few days before.

We rejoice that he had heard the Good News.

Why Are You So Old?

One time when we were visiting Spain, I went with Maria Ester Eddy to pick up her daughters from school. We also picked up the Barnreuther boy, age eight. I was then age seventy-seven.

That boy looked at me and asked, "Why are you so old?"

I didn't know how to answer such a question, but I told him, "Because I was born many years ago."

Where Is That Fantastic Woman?

It was in the year 1997. Elida and I were traveling to Spain on Continental Airlines. We were traveling on buddy passes.

On a previous Continental flight, we had met Kathy Hobbs, the sixth senior Continental flight attendant. We had become great friends. With her arrangement on a buddy pass, Kathy had to accompany us on the international route.

Kathy met us at Newark for this flight to Madrid. She told us that if there was one seat available in First Class, it would be for Gordon. If there were two seats, they would be for Elida and Gordon. If there were three seats, all three of us would be up there. On this particular flight, there was one seat, and I enjoyed it.

Sitting next to me was a businessman, a man of Indian decent. He was a Harvard MBA who was on his way to Madrid to assist a small telephone company on how to compete with Telefonica Hispanica, the largest phone company in Spain.

We talked about many things, but mostly about our wives. I kept telling him about the most fantastic woman that God ever created, Elida Barnett.

After much time, he asked, "Where is that fantastic woman?"

It was difficult to tell him the she was in the back of the aircraft in tourist class.

Then I told him about Kathy Hobbs' decision.

Magda, a Beautiful Polish Girl

It was during the year 1998; Elida and I were flying on Continental from Newark to Houston. We were coming home from Spain. We were flying on buddy passes, which meant we were flying space-available. I was in the middle seat in one row. Elida was in another middle seat.

On my right, in the aisle seat, was a beautiful young twenty-one-year-old Polish blond who was on her first flight in the USA. She was on her way to Weber State University where she had a scholarship. She was a Mormon.

I started the conversation by saying, "I am married to the most fantastic woman that God ever created."

She answered, "Someday, I hope one man will say that about me."

We talked about many things and finally I told her about a little booklet that changed my life. I asked her if I could share it with her.

She said, "Of course."

I then shared *The Four Spiritual Laws* with her. Then I asked her if she would pray the prayer. She did and was so glad that she did.

After she graduated from Weber State, she married a fellow classmate, a man from Switzerland.

They went first to Poland to visit her parents. Then they went to Switzerland to live.

She sent us photos that were taken in Venice, Italy, where they celebrated their first wedding anniversary.

We have kept in contact with Magda to this very day. She invited us to visit them when we were in Switzerland in May 2006, but we were unable to do so.

A Great VA Doctor

I met Dr. James O. Moore, an internist, a VA doctor, my primary care physician, when I visited the VA for the first time in February 1992. I had heard tales about the VA medical system, and I had been afraid to go, although I knew that I had complete VA benefits.

Within two hours after my arrival at the VA hospital in San Antonio, I had received the following: a VA ID card, one tooth pulled (with further dental appointments), two pairs of glasses ordered, ostomy equipment, and a visit with Dr. Moore.

Dr. Moore told me that he was my primary care physician, that if I was not satisfied with any care at the VA hospital, I was to contact him. He gave me his e-mail address and his phone number.

Later, when we traveled to Spain, I was running out of ostomy supplies, I e-mailed Dr. Moore and asked him to ask the supply people at the VA to FedEx supplies to me in Madrid. They told him that they couldn't send supplies out of the USA.

He then asked them to give him the supplies, and he would get them to me. He spent $65 to FedEx them, and they arrived the next day.

When we turned, we tried to repay him. He refused to take it. We then gave his wife, Martha, Cracker Barrel gift certificates.

He and Martha attended my seventy-fifth birthday party. He gave me seventeen baby chicks. They were delivered to a family in Cambodia who started a family farm.

They also attended my eightieth birthday party. This time he gave me seventeen baby ducks.

We spent Christmas at their home in 2009, and I am honored to be considered a grandpa to their kids.

How great it is to have a doctor who cares!

My Dermatologist

It was during the year 1992. Elida and I had just moved to Texas from Spain. I had skin cancer and have had it treated for years.

I went to an appointment at the large Air Force medical center called Wilford Hall (WHMC). They put me in a small room.

Shortly, a cute female came into the room with a stethoscope wrapped around her neck. She said, "I am your doctor. What do we need to do?"

I said, "Usually, I strip completely, and you burn off all the skin cancers that you can find, but you are a girl."

That doctor then said, "Commander, I have been a flight surgeon to forty-five F-16 fighter pilots for the past two years. Are you different than them?"

I answered no. She gave me a towel and told me to put it wherever I wanted to. She became a very good friend to Elida and to me.

MARIA ESTER:
A GREAT FATHER-DAUGHTER RELATIONSHIP

Maria Ester was the daughter of a Spanish Pastor. Elida and I had known her since she was sixteen years old.

Bill Eddy, a missionary in Spain, met Maria in Motril, Spain, during a decision campaign. They dated, fell in love, and were soon engaged to be married.

Maria's father, being the Pastor that he was, not only walked her down the aisle, but also performed the marriage ceremony.

We will never forget the moment as father and daughter were walking down the aisle when, in the hushed and solemn presence of an overcrowded church, the groom suddenly blurted out to his bride-to-be, "Have I ever told you that you are beautiful?"

This unexpected exuberant expression of love and devotion resulted in the entire congregation breaking out in laughter.

Years later when Elida and I were visiting Spain, Maria Ester's father died. At the conclusion of the funeral, Maria threw her arms around my neck and cried, "I don't have a daddy anymore. Would you be my daddy?"

Overcome with emotion, I replied, "Yes, I would try."

Our next visit to Spain was shortly after my own daughter's death from pancreatic cancer. When I encountered Maria, I hugged her as she did me at her father's funeral, and I cried, "My baby daughter has died. Would you be my daughter?" With sincere reciprocation, she also replied that she would try.

And, for the last twelve years, we have had a beautiful father-daughter relationship.

DEATH OF TWO CHILDREN

My second son, David, took his own life on June 25, 1974. He was twenty-five years old. His suicide occurred during my alcoholic days. I dove deeper into the bottle to drown my grief. I know that my alcoholic life was a major contributor to his death. My alcoholism was also most likely the factor in the breakup of my marriage.

It was a very sad time in my life. My drinking continued, and my depression became deeper. I considered taking the same direction to end my life, but my religious background and the thought of going to hell kept me from doing the deed. This was another moment in my life when my mother's prayers and my Jesus protected me.

My life was quite different when my daughter, Darla, died of pancreatic cancer on February 10, 1997. She was forty-five years old. She was my baby daughter.

At this time of sorrow, I had committed my life to Jesus Christ and His grace brought comfort to my heart. The prayers and support of my friends and especially of my precious wife, Elida, supported me as I grieved.

In the death of my two children, the journey of grief was similarly painful, but, as the verse from the wonderful hymn "He Giveth More Grace" states, "He giveth more grace as our burdens grow greater, He sendeth more strength as our labors increase. To added affliction He addeth His mercy. To multiplied trials He multiplies peace . . . His love has no limits, His grace has no measure . . . For out of His infinite riches in Jesus, He giveth, and giveth, and giveth again."

Those words comforted me as I processed Darla's death, and they became a reality to me.

As we were going to press with this book, I received a message from a spiritual daughter, my dental hygienist.

Gordon, Congratulations on your new book that is coming out soon. I can't wait to read it.

I am so blessed to have had you come into my life ten years ago and when our Jesus changed me from a lost girl to a King's Daughter.

You may have lost 2 children of your own, but you gained me and many other children of God because you cared enough to reach out and help win a lost soul.

I can never thank you enough for changing my life for the better. I will never forget your kindness and love.

I love you! Michele

THE WORD *BEAUTIFUL*

It was during the year 1996. We were living in San Antonio. The largest grocery stores in San Antonio were called H-E-Bs.

The lady at the cash register in this particular H-E-B had accepted my payment and had bagged my groceries. She was about sixty years of age.

As I was leaving, I turned around and said to her, "You are beautiful." She broke down in tears.

I asked her, "Did I do anything wrong?"

When she was able to talk, she said, "I have not heard that word for twenty years."

BENJAMIN

He was only eight years old. He lived in Phoenix, Arizona. He visited us in San Antonio the weekend of March 15, 2008. He was with his sister, Hannah, age ten, and his mother, Luisa Ogan.

Luisa had found Jesus Christ in Spain when she was fifteen years old. It was a result of Elida's life and testimony.

Benjamin didn't walk in our home; he hopped like a kangaroo. The house shook whenever he was present.

Elida took him to the local army base, Fort San Houston. In the BX, she purchased an army uniform that fitted him perfectly.

The Ogans departed San Antonio for Dallas on March 16. Before they left, I had Benjamin practice the hand salute. He did it perfectly. I told him that he had to salute all military personnel in uniform because he would always be the most junior.

His mother called us after they arrived in Dallas. She said that he saluted every military person in the San Antonio Airport and in the Dallas Airport and that every single one of them returned the salute. How patriotic can you be?

MY ENCOUNTER WITH A FOUR-STAR GENERAL

My brother Bev served with him at Vandenberg AFB. My friend, Col. John Wright, taught him to fly the B-58 when John was a Captain. Both told me he was a firm, stern general. He is Gen. P. K. Carlton. I call him PK1.

I met him at Scott AFB where Elida was hospitalized for abdominal surgery. The surgeon was Dr. P. K. Carlton, PK2. It was after a chapel service when PK2 introduced me to PK1.

I said to PK1, "I am your competitor."

He answered firmly, "I have no competition."

I then said, "I have a paper that says that I am an honorary grandfather to your grandchildren. Can you prove that you are their grandfather?"

He smiled. We have been friends since.

HERB ALLEN, A MAN I ONCE HATED, I NOW LOVE

During the year 1974, my wife Phyllis divorced me and married Herb Allen. I believe that my alcoholism contributed to the divorce. I was not a good husband, nor was I a good father. I hated Herb, and I also hated my ex-wife. At that time, I could not accept any of the blame for the divorce. Now I know that I was responsible.

I later found Elida and married her on May 2, 1978.

On September 15, 1978, Elida and I accepted Jesus Christ as our Savior in our home at a Bible study.

During September 2007, I wrote a snail mail letter to Herb Allen. I told him that he had taken a girl that I had injured and had nursed her back to health, that he had loved my children as his own, and that he had loved my grandchildren as his own. I then told him that he was one of my heroes.

Three months later, in December 2007, we found out that Herb Allen had pancreatic cancer and had from two to five months to live.

I sent him another snail mail letter telling him how to accept Jesus Christ as his personal Savior. I did not expect an answer and received none.

Just before Christmas 2007, my son Doug and his wife, Lisa, traveled to San Diego to visit with his mother and stepfather, Herb Allen. On departing San Diego, Doug hugged Herb and told him that he loved him. Herb told Doug that he loved him too. Then Herb whispered in Doug's ear, "I have made peace with Jesus, but don't tell your dad." I rejoiced when I heard the good news. Herb died in December 2008.

HOW TO LOVE YOUR WIFE

In August 2009, I was asked to speak at a men's reunion. I was given the title of the speech. It was "How to Love Your Wife." This is how it goes:

How to Love Your Wife

I am married to the most fantastic woman that God ever created. My great desire is to love her as Christ loves her. I want her to be the most loved of all the women in the world.

Ephesians 5:25 says, "Love your wife . . ."

1 Corinthians 7:3 says, "Let the husband render to his wife the affection due her . . ."

I did not love Elida when we married. I was an alcoholic. Alcoholics can love nothing, except themselves and their alcohol. I married her because she would not talk to me unless I married her.

I had ruined a previous marriage and caused a suicide of a son—mainly because of my drinking. Four months after our marriage, we accepted Jesus Christ as our Lord and Savior.

I was unable to stop drinking. I was living a defeated life. I was a closet drinker. Elida prayed me into alcohol rehabilitation. With God's help and with the help of AA, I gained control of my drinking. Life then became beautiful.

Eight years after our marriage, we attended Amsterdam 86. It was a Billy Graham outreach to ten thousand evangelists and two thousand stewards. There I heard Josh McDowell talk on "how to be a hero to your kids."

During his presentation, he often referred to a lady in the front row as "the most fantastic woman that God ever created." Every time he said that, she beamed, and I got shivers up my spine.

I thought that I must try that, and since that time, I have referred to my wife as *the most fantastic woman that God ever created.*

Elida was a great wife before, but from then on, she became more fantastic. The more fantastic she became, the deeper was the love that I had for her.

The circle grew larger because the deeper my love became, the more perfect she became. I know that I helped her.

Some would say that we are not compatible

We don't drink the same kind of coffee.
We don't drink the same kind of milk.
She wants her Coke with sugar. I want mine without.
I get up early in the morning, she loves to sleep in.
She likes Chester's Hamburgers, I prefer Fuddruckers.
She likes Blue Bell ice cream, I like Bryers.
I am run by a stopwatch, she is run by a calendar.
She likes space movies. I don't

I enjoy listening to Rush Limbaugh, she doesn't. She squeezes the middle of a toothpaste tube, I don't. We even use different kinds of toilet paper.

We are happily incompatible. Because of that, we have a great marriage. You can ask her, and she will tell you the same.

We have the freedom to be different and not feel guilty. Our personal differences keep life interesting and exciting.

YOUR BEST WITNESS FOR OUR JESUS IS YOUR MARRIAGE

How you treat your wife, how you speak to her, how you touch her, and how you listen to her is the greatest way to witness. I am a novelty in this community because I love my wife, and everybody knows it. Isn't that weird?

PRIORITIES

A few years ago, the WSJ had an article about *priorities*.

They said that a person whose first priority was their God, second priority was their wife, third priority was their children, and fourth priority was their career was a person who had a balanced life. That person would have the most successful career.

In my working life, my first priority was my career because I had no God. I suppose that my second was my wife and the third was my children.

The result: Two of my sons were on heavy drugs. My daughter was living with a man not her husband. One son put a rifle in his mouth and shot his brains out. My wife divorced me. Maybe the WSJ was correct. I was a terrible husband and father.

GOOD NEWS

Today, two of my children are in heaven and the other three have committed their lives to our Jesus.

FORGIVENESS

The most important ingredient to cause the honeymoon to go on forever is not *love*, is not *communication*, is not *compatibility*, is not respect, It is *forgiveness*. If you don't forgive, resentment sets in, then communication stops, then the marriage is almost dead.

We have a marriage staff meeting once a week. It is at a time when we are both relaxed. It could be on one of our dates. At that time, we can bear our souls.

Do you put the TV on mute whenever your wife starts to speak? If you don't, you have slapped her in the face because you have told her that the TV is more important than she is.

Do you drop the newspaper and look directly at her whenever she or one of your children speak to you? If you don't, you have slapped them in the face.

Stealing is not limited to a tangible object. It could be the theft of time, energy, or attention, which rightfully belongs to your wife.

You are in your office. A very important client is in your office, and your wife calls you on the phone. Do you tell the client that it is my wife and she is the most important person in the world and you take the call?

If you do, I promise that your client will give you respect and remain you client. The same goes for a phone call from your child. What are your priorities?

LET'S TALK ABOUT SEX

Sex is better at eighty-six than it was when I was twenty-five because I am a better husband.

When I married Elida, I was a great-grandfather. Shortly after we married, we purchased a sex book by the Christian author, Tim LaHaye, *The Act of Marriage*. It was a great investment.

God designed sex to help a man and his wife to get closer and to be and live in oneness. Having babies was secondary. If not that way, we would make love to our wives at the most twenty times during our life.

Sex does not start in the bedroom. It starts in the kitchen. It starts a day or even two days before the act.

Kevin Leman said, "Sexually pursue your wife outside the bedroom. Good sex is an all-day affair. You can't treat your wife like a servant and expect her to be eager to sleep with you at night. Your wife's sexual responsiveness will be determined by how willingly you help out with the dishes, the kids' homework, or that leaky faucet that drips.

"This is difficult for many men to understand, in large part, because we remove sex from every other part of our life. We think sex fixes things on its own—but it doesn't do that for a woman. The context, the history, the current level of emotional closeness—all that directly affects your wife's desire and enjoyment of sexual relations. A good lover works just as hard outside the bedroom as he does inside it."

My desire is to make love to my wife every day. I treat her with gentleness, tenderness, and kindness. I want to listen to all that she has to say.

I touch her lovingly. I hug her tenderly. My goal every day is to be so nice to her that she will melt in my arms. Come to think of it, that is not a bad way to treat her all of the time.

Do I make love to her every day? No, but I make love to her more often than if I had called her *stupid* all day long.

If you are not bringing your wife to at least one orgasm every time that you make love, you are failing. Either you didn't start yesterday, there was not enough foreplay before the act, or you are exploding too soon.

You can correct all of these problems. If you are exploding too soon, slow down your stroke, even to almost no motion. It is tantalizing to your wife, and it prolongs your endurance. Her satisfaction should be your most important goal. Every orgasm she has is a golden gift to you. Remember, you caused it, but she gave it.

Men, the most important time in your wife's life is the time after complete satisfaction by both you and your wife.

The words that you first say, she will remember for the rest of her life. So always make those words precious. Extreme gentleness is necessary at this time.

She will remember such things as your hands that lovingly touch her, your tone of voice that expresses caring, and your smile that lights her up.

Also for the thirty minutes to one hour after complete satisfaction, she needs and wants your body next to hers. That is part of the act of love.

When you married your wife, the perfect Hollywood female body was moved into your bedroom.

Her breasts are perfect, her legs are perfect, and her butt is perfect. Let her know daily that God created a perfect body when he created her.

Tell her so many times that when you see porno on your computer monitor, it will nauseate you. Why shouldn't you set the standard instead of Hollywood setting it? In this area, nothing is as strong as gentleness.

At age seventy-five, I needed a little help, and some genius created Viagra. When you use Viagra, they tell you to wait for one hour after you take the pill before penetration.

What are you going to do for one hour after a passionate woman gives you the little blue pill?

Foreplay is the answer. I will bet that none of you have ever had one hour of foreplay with your wife. I never did before Viagra. Try the one hour of foreplay sometime. You will have a beautiful day. We men are always in a hurry to start the action.

A man whose first priority is the satisfaction of his wife is a great lover. A man whose first priority is his own satisfaction is a lousy lover.

Ted Roberts in the new May 2003 *Man's Magazine* states, "If you ask the average woman to list her intimacy needs, you would probably find that 80 to 90% of her needs are met simply by being held or cuddled.

"For the average guy, however, sexual intercourse is the only item on the list."

SOME DOs

1. Let the first words that she hears when you arise in the morning be "*I love you.*" Let the last words that she hears before she goes to sleep be "*I love you.*" May she be enveloped with that phrase all day long.

2. Let her have complete freedom to be her natural self. Do not smother her with your requirements. Listen and listen well. Give her time to share what it is in her heart.

3. At least once a week, say to your wife, "I really like it when you *****." She will repeat that thing because she also wants to please you.

4. Are you aware that your wife has many needs? You must nourish your wife mentally, physically, emotionally, and spiritually. She needs to know that you notice and appreciate her struggles.

5. Give her one gram of love, she will give you one kilo in return. Quite often in front of your children, her parents, and other friends, let them know what

a fantastic wife/mother/friend that she is. Never stop because you are her encourager.

7. Tell her often, "I am pleased with you." These words are very important in a marriage relationship. The words, "I am pleased with you not just for what you do, but for who you are," can make your partner's day so much brighter.

8. Listen to her, not just with your ears, but with your heart.

9. Pray with your wife daily. Listen when she prays. You will learn what is troubling her. Read God's word together daily.

10. Continually give her appreciation. Thank her for each meal that she prepares for you. Thank her for a clean home. Thank her for being a great mother. Do this daily.

11. Accept each other unconditionally, and our Jesus will prompt and empower needed changes.

12. If something is important to your wife, if it is within reason, make certain that it is important to you, also.

13. Daily homework: twice a day, hold your wife completely in your arms, nonsexually, for one minute.

You can whisper sweet nothings in her ear during this time if you wish. It works best when the children are around. Do this hours apart, preferably near the beginning of the day and near the end of the day.

14. Monthly homework: Ask your wife, "On a scale of 1 to 10, how would you rate our marriage?"

   Your wife knows the answer, we men never do. Whatever her answer, whether it is a 7 or an 8, then ask her, "What must I do to make it a 10?"

   Then consider in your heart what she says. You will be shocked how much better your marriage will be.

   Homework will be passed out to each of you men at the close of this meeting.

16. Your statements and beliefs about your partner will help to shape that person. One way you can do this is through affirmation.

17. My last DO. If harmony in your home is lacking, try this: For one month, defer to her by extending priority to all of her desires. Let her be right all of the time. Serve her by loving her.

This is one way of nurturing your wife. It will cost you a little of your pride. If you enjoy the harmony that this produces, continue for another month.

You will notice how much more she will respect you. She will listen to you with much more enthusiasm.

She will start to attend to you more than ever before. She will not look down at you for this consideration. She will love the new you.

SOME DON'Ts

1. There never is a correct time to criticize your wife. Also, never criticize your children. There is a time to tell her, "Let me show you a better way." There is a substitute for criticism. It is called love. More changes occur with love than with criticism.

2. Never use the word, *divorce*, even in jest. If your child tells you that the parents of a friend are getting a divorce, *immediately* sit your family down and look at the faces of your children and speak with emphasis, "I never will leave your mother!" Say it again, and again, then hug your wife and kids in a football huddle and continue to say it.

3. Never argue with your wife in front of your children.

4. After any argument with your wife, and it will happen, if you spoke in an unkind way to your wife, you must be the first to ask, "Forgive me?"

Even if your were right in the argument and your wife was wrong, you be the first. You are asking forgiveness for speaking unkindly to your wife.

You are the spiritual leader in the home, and you are to set the example.

5. Remove the word, *why*, from your home. That word is for the classroom, not the home. It is almost impossible to answer a *why* question. It also hurts to be asked that question.

6. Don't have any rules for your wife. Have them for yourself and for the children, but not for that precious diamond who shares your home.

7. Don't *rush* your wife. It is OK to say to her, "We should probably depart in fifteen minutes." From then on, never mention time again. It is better to arrive five minutes late as sweethearts than to arrive on time in war clouds.

    Now is the time to say to her, "How can I help you?" She probably won't ask you to do anything, but just the thought of you wanting to help will calm her.

8. Don't sweat the small stuff.

    My father had a rule that we must never leave a room with the light on. It became a habit for me.

    Elida was raised in a home where the electricity bill was not important. She loves to have brilliance around her at all times. Therefore she always left the lights on.

I continually told her to turn off the lights when she left a room. Soon it became an irritant, and voices were raised.

I realized that if she left the light on all night long, the cost would be about four cents. I asked myself, "Is an argument worth four cents?"

Peace in our family is worth much more than four cents.

From then on, every time I turned off the light, I thanked our Jesus for Elida, for her presence, and for her love.

She is *the light of my life*.

Do I, Gordon Barnett, do all of the above? No, but I try. When I fail, I ask her to forgive me.

DAVID ROBINSON

At the Hall of Fame dinner, David Robinson took a few minutes during his acceptance speech to offer a tribute to his wife.

"Without her, there is no me. She has refined me," he said. "Whatever I have become over the years is because of her. I love you, Valerie."

Have you ever honored your wife like that?

I tell you a story about Robertson and Muriel McQuilkin. Robert was the president of Columbia Bible College and his wife, Muriel, was a well-known speaker at various women's gatherings and retreats.

Their lives were blossoming, and they were loved by all who knew them and many who didn't.

At Robert's age of fifty-seven, Muriel developed Alzheimer's and became dependent on Robert for everything.

Robert resigned his position to spend twenty-four hours a day taking care of Muriel. He was asked, "Why don't you put her in a home for Alzheimer's? She doesn't know you."

He answered, "She doesn't know me, but I know who she is. I don't have to take care of Muriel. I get to take care of her."

A few years ago, when Elida and I were in Columbia, SC, we saw them at sunset, walking hand in hand among the trees. It was the most perfect picture of love that we had ever seen.

Would you do this for your wife?

We can watch the soft skin of our partner slowly turn to wrinkles. But instead of turning away, we can choose instead to see the love that which resides within her.

You have been given a two-billion-dollar diamond. You have two choices. Hold it carefully, polish it, and let it shine back at you.

Or you can throw it on the ground, kick it as far as you can. Walk up to it and kick it again and again. You are doing one or the other. There is no in between.

I have no advice for a wife. I believe that if she is treated correctly, she will respond perfectly. It is up to you guys.

If you knew she would die tomorrow, would you treat her differently today?

WOULD YOU DIE FOR YOUR WIFE? DOES SHE KNOW IT?

MY FINAL SPEECH TO MY SQUADRON

Forty-six (46) years after I relinquished my command and turned VP-4 over to CDR. Mo Moses, I was the speaker at the final banquet at our squadron reunion in Fort Worth, Texas, in October 2009. These are the words that I said to the officers and enlisted men of VP-4:

You guys were the greatest!

I am married to the most fantastic woman that God ever created. Her name is Elida. If you get too close to her, she will bless you.
I checked on the history of VP-4 and found the following on the Internet:

Starting a longstanding tradition of excellence, in 1964, VP-4 marked its fourth year of unequaled operational excellence with

3 Commander Naval Air Forces Pacific Navy "E" Ribbons

3 Chief of Naval Operations (CNO) Safety Awards

4 Arnold J. Isbell ASW Awards.

No other VP squadron in Naval history can claim such a record.

I was fortunate to have served in VP-4 during two of each of those awards. Some of you here tonight served during three of them.

In the early spring of 1962, as XO of VP-31, the Pacific Fleet replacement squadron at North Island, I received a phone call from the chief of staff of AIRPAC. He asked me if I was going to register at San Diego State University for the spring semester. I told him that I was. He warned me not to, but he would not tell me why. I told him that if he wouldn't tell me why, I would register. He then said, "You are receiving orders to VP-4 as the new CO." I fell out of my chair. I did not even know that I had been screened for command.

I had heard many stories about VP-4 and I didn't believe them. No squadron could be that good. I had hoped that if I got to command a squadron, it would be a squadron at the bottom of the list, not the top. How can you improve on the best?

After I arrived at Naha, I went over the squadron orders with Scotty Edmonds, the man I was to relieve. The VP-4 recall list listed a Madam Umagutchi in Naminue as one of the people to call. I told Scotty, "How can you do this?" He told me to try it.

I did, for one midnight, I called the SDO and told him to execute the squadron recall and that quarters would be fifteen minutes early that morning. One man missed it. I left Madam Umagutchi in Naminue on the recall list.

I did not need to be in VP-4, but just a short time when I found out that the stories about VP-4 were true. The more I observed, the more I was shocked about how great were the officers and men in VP-4.

To be the skipper of VP-4 during 1962-63 was like riding 410 mustangs at the same time. The ride was rough, but it was fun.

I don't know whether the officers and men got the VP-4 disease before they arrived or after they got there, but it was a disease.

I had served in four VP squadrons and all were awarded the coveted Navy Battle Efficiency "E." None of them could hold a candle to VP-4.

You guys were the greatest!

Harvey McKay tells the story of a professor who stood before a class of thirty senior molecular biology students.

Before he passed out the final exam, he stated, "I have been privileged to be your instructor this semester, and I know how hard you have worked to prepare for this test. I also know that most of you are off to medical school or grad school next fall. I am well aware of how much pressure you are under to keep your grade point average up, and because I am so confident that you know this material that I am prepared to offer an automatic B to anyone who opts to skip taking the final exam."

The relief was audible. A number of students jumped up from their desks, thanking their professor for the lifeline he had thrown them.

"Any other takers?" he asked. "This is your last opportunity."

One more student decided to go.

The instructor then handed out the final exam, which consisted of two sentences. "Congratulations," it read, "you just received an A in this class. Keep believing in yourself."

There were 55 officers and 355 men in VP-4 who would have stayed and taken the exam.

I inherited a fantastic squadron. About the only thing that I changed was that I got rid of one piece of paper.

It was the one that the enlisted men needed to get signed in order to get a day off. He needed to get the signatures of four or five persons before he could take his wife to the doctor. I believe they were the division chief, the division officer, the leading chief, and possibly the XO.

My new order was that he had to request permission only from his division chief and then he was to leave. His division chief then replaced him in the shop, the flight schedule, and the watch schedule.

Our officers and men were cocky. Our duty driver had a sign that he put in the duty pickup. It read, "My name is Brawn and I am the best damn duty driver in the Navy."

At Captain's mast, I would always ask the division chief and the division officer what this man was like in the division. If they would vouch for him, the man would get a warning. If they couldn't, he would get the maximum punishment that I could give. All the men soon learned that the skipper did not set the sentence; it was set by their division chief and/or their division officer.

If a man had been picked up for fighting and was brought to mast, he would usually say, "Skipper, the other man said that VP-4 was not the best." Whether the facts were true or not, this man certainly got a *warning*.

You guys were the greatest.

These are some of the great achievements that you guys accomplished while I was there. You guys did it, and I thank you very much.

1. Two Battle Efficiency "E" Awards
2. Two CNO Safety Awards
3. Two Arnold J. Isbell ASW Awards
4. The highest first-term reenlistment rate of all twenty-five VP squadrons
5. You outflew all twenty-five VP squadrons in the world.
6. You transitioned from P2V5s to P2V7s on Okinawa without missing an operational commitment.
7. You had the lowest VD rate among all deployed VP squadrons. (Don't ask me how you people accomplished this.)
8. The only way that you knew it was a Sunday was that there were no doughnuts in the ready room.
9. You guys had the most beautiful wives of all the VP squadrons.

I received unsolicited letters from the skippers of two nuclear atomic attack submarines.

I quote from commanding officer, USS *Grudgeon* (SS-567) dated April 7, 1963, "For the second time this WESTPAC tour it has been *Grudgeon*'s extreme pleasure to have rendered her services to your outstanding squadron. Your aircraft were on station the entire operating period. The attacks made were from excellent to outstanding.

Commanding Officer *Grudgeon* wishes to state that in his submarine experience covering a period of fourteen years, he has never had the pleasure of working with a finer airborne ASW outfit. Many of the other squadrons could not even find us.

The spirit and eagerness which your pilots displayed and the manner in which they conducted the exercises are exceptional. We congratulate you on winning your second "E" and, from our viewpoint, consider that you are well on your way to a third one. We hope that if we ever go to war that you guys will be on our side. Signed, W. W. McKenzie Jr."

A quote from Commanding Officer USS *Razorback* (SS-394) dated April 17, 1963, "It is always a pleasure to work with a group who know what they are doing and having worked with most of them VP squadrons in the Pacific, I know how RARE it is. Good hunting! M. E. Davis"

I don't know of any other VP squadron that received one letter of commendation from the CO of a nuclear attack submarine.

You guys were the greatest.

We had many all stars in VP-4. The brightest of all of them was a second-class petty officer named David Bonnett.

He was the lead tech in my crew, and he was the director of the new ASCAC that we had started shortly before. Many of us thought that he was indispensable.

We were offering all sorts of promises to him if he would reenlist, but he seemed determined to leave the Navy.

One Sunday, I was in my Quonset hut office, in walked Dave and another sailor. They had had a few drinks and were extremely happy. They were not drunk.

Dave greeted me with the words, "Skipper, I want to re-enlist right now."

I told him, "Bonnett, come back tomorrow and we will do it."

Mo Moses, our XO, was mad because we didn't do it right then. He wanted to have Dave Bonnett, because Mo would be the CO in about one month.

Dave did come back the next day, and he brought his brother, Bill. We reenlisted both of them.

Shortly after that, we were able to send both of them to college in the Navy NESEP program. Dave went on to become a nuclear scientist. Bill, his brother, retired as a Navy Captain.

The Bonnett brothers were of great benefit to the Navy.

Other all-stars that served with me were

Bob Zafran
Bill Conroy

Steve Andruszkewicz
Richard Douglas
Bob Douty
Norman Kleno
William Guempelein
Clay Riecher
David Adams
Bob McKee (now in heaven)

There were many more, and if I have forgotten your name, remember, I am eighty-five, and I have senior moments, so please forgive.

The pilots in VP-4 could not agree who was our best *aviator*. All were great. I will settle that now. Chuck Doughdrill was our best *aviator*. He is here tonight.

My greatest fear was that I would have to send a death message to a next of kin. I had a sample that I personalized in my center desk drawer. Thank God, I never had to send it.

Regrets

1. I regret that I didn't have one year as XO of VP-4 before I was the CO. Being in VP-4 was such an honor and privilege. One year was not enough. I needed more time to know the officers and men.

2. I regret that I was not more relaxed as the skipper. I could have enjoyed the journey more if I had been relaxed.

3. I regret that I did not take the NATOPS check flight that I had Art Schloffman, Sam Walker, and Chuck Doughdrill take. I helped write the NATOPS manual while in VP-31; I had been instructing NATOPS procedures. I should have taken it.

Because Lockheed had made me a great job offer to be their ASW plans and programming officer, I retired from the Navy after leaving VP-4. You guys were so great, and Lockheed gave me the credit for it. When I was halfway out, Lockheed called me and told me that they were going for the supersonic transport and could not hire any more executives.

I went into business and was very successful until alcohol took over my life. I became a full-blown alcoholic. As a result of my alcoholism, Phyllis divorced me, and my son David took his life.

I traveled to Europe on Space-A. My first space-available flight took me to Torrejon Air Base just outside Madrid, Spain. I lived in Madrid, and five years later, I put an ad in the newspaper just to meet more women. Elida thought that it was an ad for a job. She answered my ad, and on the interview, we talked about our lives. Thirty days later, she proposed to me, and I said no. Four days later, I said yes. This was on March 17, 1978.

Six months later, we committed our lives to Jesus Christ. Wow! What a different life for me.

We remained in Spain for fourteen years as lay missionaries and came here to San Antonio in 1992. I worked with alcoholics in Spain. I work with them today.

I celebrated my seventy-fifth birthday eleven years ago. My oldest son, Dennis, who used to be ashamed of me, sent me these words, "My prayers used to be 'O God, do something about my dad.' Now I pray, 'O Lord, make me more like my dad.'"

Because of VP-4, my life has been touched most deeply. In VP-4, I saw men do things that were impossible. They did it day after day and night after night. They were extraordinary officers and men.

In my eighty-five years of life, I have never seen a group of officers and men work with such high morale like those did in VP-4 during '62 and '63.

I am a better man for having served with you fantastic people.

You guys were the greatest.

Epilogue

MY MOTHER

Lucy Minerva Miller Barnett was her name. She had seven sons and one daughter. I was her prodigal son. I gave her more problems that all of the rest combined. I caused my mother's hair to turn white.

Although I was her problem child, she made me feel like I was her favorite. I believe that each of her children thought that they were her favorite.

Her love touched my life in such a special way. She prayed for me for 54 years before her prayers were answered. Although she is in heaven, I thank her now for those prayers.

47 years APART

Elida and I visited Oahu Hawaii during November 2009 to celebrate my 86th birthday. While there we visited the Commanding Officer of VP-4, CDR Jack Thomas USN, which is home ported at Kaneohe. We both Commanded VP-4, 47 years apart.
Afterward we exchanged e-mails which are now quoted.

The one hour that we spent with you and your staff was a key moment in my life.
Thank you for the honor and respect that you and your people displayed. It is obvious that fire in the belly is still burning in your outstanding squadron.

Gordon Barnett

. . . .

Skipper,
Seeing the obvious impact that your time in VP-4 had on you caused me to reaffirm the impact it is having in my life as well.
You gave me an opportunity to appreciate the things I have before they are gone.
That is a rare gift that I wish more people had. Now I have a six-month head start on being grateful.

Cheers, Jack Thomas

. . . .

Jack, you have just written the script for the movie, IT'S A WONDERFUL LIFE" with James Stewart. We like to watch it every Christmas time.

I have been a good predictor of Naval Officer Promotions. You will wear Stars in the future, but your time with VP-4 will contain the greatest moments of your life. Enjoy them!

"On our last night, we attended a Hawaiian Luau. There were about 200 military people present. Most had grey hair. Near the end of the program, they asked all WWII Veterans to stand. I stood. I looked all around from left to right. I was shocked.
I WAS ALONE.
Many people came up to me, shook my hand and said, "Thank you".
Wow! I was alive. They are dying at the rate of 1000 per day, I was told".

Gordon Barnett

My Doxology

I have been one of the most fortunate men that I know.

I have been down, and I have been up. My downs were as a result of my own choices, and I hold myself accountable and have asked and received forgiveness. My successes have been partly due to my determined resolve and religious upbringing, but mainly a result of my mother's prayers and the encouragement from others.

My health is good (in spite of my drinking and smoking and earlier serious medical conditions).

My friends are many today. There was a time in my life when there were few. My guilt is gone. I have been forgiven. I know where I will go when I die.

My children, who once were ashamed of me, now respect me.

I am married to the most fantastic woman that God ever created.

Sometimes, I truly believe that I am God's favorite.

My advice to others is to attempt the difficult hurdles, face challenges, and don't worry about failing. Time is all you have. And you will find one day that you have less time than you think. Pray much and follow the teachings of the Bible.

Although I am eighty-six and my health is great, I have been contemplating my eventual passage to my Lord's heaven and have been making preparations for my death.

I have thought about what I would do if I had one hour to live.

If I had one hour to live, I would not call my banker, my lawyer, my doctor, my stockbroker, or my insurance company.

I would not need to call anyone and ask for forgiveness, for I keep that account paid up.

I would not have to give my beloved Elida any instructions, for they have already been written out.

I would call my children, and I would tell them how much they mean to me and how much they have blessed my life, and moreover, how much I love them.

Then I would hold Elida in my arms for the remaining minutes of the final hour.

Until then, I then shall live as one who has been forgiven.

About the Author

Gordon Richard Barnett was born November 29, 1923, at Penn Run, Pennsylvania, a village near Indiana, Pennsylvania, to Clarence Henry and Lucy Minerva Barnett. His father was a Wesleyan Methodist Pastor. His parents had eight children: seven boys and one girl. Gordon was child number two.

The family moved to Iowa, where his father pastored churches near Cedar Rapids, in Independence, near La Porte City, near Sloan, and in Rudd.

Gordon attended Miltonvale Wesleyan Academy in Miltonvale, Kansas, for his high school, which he completed in three years.

The Barnett family moved to Houghton, New York, where Gordon attended Houghton College for two and a half years until the World War II draft was about to take him into the army. When the orders came for the military physical, Gordon enlisted in the Navy's aviation cadet program.

On a thirty-day leave after his commissioning, he met and married Phyllis Arlene Whitney from Jackson, Michigan. She was also a student at Houghton College.

He began his torpedo pilot training and served in three Navy torpedo squadrons. He was cross-trained as a patrol plane pilot. Subsequently he served in four Navy patrol squadrons, the last being VP-4, home ported at Naha, Okinawa, which he commanded. All four of his VP squadrons were awarded the coveted Navy Battle Efficiency "E."

Gordon retired in 1963 as a Commander after twenty-one years of service.

Gordon ventured into the life insurance business with the Prudential Life Insurance Company. He was successful and immediately became a large producer. He was a member of the Million Dollar Round Table.

When alcohol took over his life, his son committed suicide, and his wife divorced him, he left the sales field and wandered aimlessly, traveling around the world mostly throughout Europe. One of his destinations was Spain, where five years later, he met and married Elida Cristina Lesconzo Adames on May 2, 1978.

On September 15, 1978, Gordon and Elida committed their lives to Jesus Christ. It was on his mother's eightieth birthday. They stayed in Spain as lay missionaries and moved to San Antonio, Texas, in January 1992.

He earned a bachelor of arts degree at San Diego State University 1963 in business management.

He earned the Chartered Life Underwriter (CLU) degree in 1969.

He earned a master of science degree at Pepperdine University in 1974 in city management and urban studies.

He and his first wife, Phyllis, were extras in a movie with John Wayne in 1956, *The Wings of Eagles*.

He tied Jesse Owens' world record in the fifty-yard dash in 1943 at Rensselaer Polytechnic Institute under Coach Wiley Knight.

He was a task group Commander (CTF72.2) with the US Navy Seventh Fleet (1962-1963).

He is the father of five children: Karen Miller, Dennis Gordon Barnett, David Bradley Barnett, Douglas Whitney Barnett, and Darla Joyce Henry.

He is a man transformed by the grace, mercy, and forgiveness of the Lord Jesus Christ.

Get Published, Inc!
Thorofare, NJ 08086
16 February, 2010
BA2010047